CHATGPT FOR COPYWRITING

HOW TO USE THE POWER OF AI TO SUPERCHARGE YOUR SIDE HUSTLE OR AGENCY AS A COPYWRITER

MARK SILVER

EMPIRE Publishing

Houston, TX

www.empireghostwriter.com/book-process

contact@empireghostwriter.com

@empirepublishing

ISBN [ebook] - 978-1-956283-68-6

ISBN [paperback] - 978-1-956283-69-3

ISBN [hardcover] -978-1-956283-70-9

CONTENTS

In this comprehensive guide, you will learn how to harness the power of ChatGPT to revolutionize your copywriting career.

From mastering the basics of copywriting to using AI for different mediums, such as advertisements, content marketing, email marketing, SEO, and social media, this book provides step-by-step guidance on leveraging ChatGPT to make more money and save time.

Overcome common challenges, stay ahead of the competition, and build a successful copywriting business in the age of AI. The future of copywriting is here, and it's powered by ChatGPT.

UNDERSTANDING THE POWER OF AI IN COPYWRITING

In this fast-paced digital era, the power of AI in copywriting cannot be underestimated. It has transformed the way businesses communicate with their target audience. Understanding its potential is crucial for any copywriter looking to thrive in the industry.

THE RISE OF AI IN COPYWRITING

The rise of AI in copywriting is a result of the rapid advancements in natural language processing and machine learning. AI-powered tools, like ChatGPT, have emerged as powerful allies for copywriters, offering a range of capabilities to enhance their writing process.

From generating ideas and outlines to improving the clarity and style of copy, AI has revolutionized the copywriting landscape.

ADVANTAGES OF AI COPYWRITING

AI copywriting offers a plethora of advantages that can significantly benefit copywriters in their quest to make more money and save time. Firstly, AI can automate repetitive tasks, allowing copywriters to focus on higher-level creative work. It can assist in generating headlines, crafting engaging introductions, and even refining the overall structure of the copy. This automation not only speeds up the writing process but also ensures consistency and quality.

Furthermore, AI tools can provide valuable insights and suggestions to optimize copy for better performance. Whether identifying potential improvements in grammar and style or recommending more persuasive language, AI acts as a writing partner that elevates the copywriter's skills and output.

OVERCOMING THE FEAR OF AUTOMATION

While the rise of AI in copywriting brings immense opportunities, it's natural to have concerns and fears surrounding automation. Many copywriters worry about technology replacing their jobs entirely. However, it's important to recognize that AI is not here to replace human creativity but to augment it.

By embracing AI as a valuable tool in your copywriting arsenal, you can leverage its capabilities to your advantage. AI can handle time-consuming tasks, freeing up your time to focus on strategic thinking, crafting compelling narratives, and building meaningful connections with your audience. It's about understanding how AI can complement your skills, making you an even more effective and successful copywriter.

In the following chapters, we'll explore how you can harness the power of AI in copywriting to supercharge your productivity, enhance your creativity, and ultimately make more money. So, let's dive deeper into the world of AI copywriting and discover the strategies and techniques that will propel your career to new heights.

MASTERING THE BASICS OF COPYWRITING

Copywriting is both an art and a science. It requires a deep understanding of human psychology, persuasive writing techniques, and the ability to connect with your target audience.

In this chapter, we will delve into the fundamental principles that will help you master the basics of copywriting and set a strong foundation for your AI-assisted writing journey.

COPYWRITING FUNDAMENTALS

To become a successful copywriter, the first step is understanding the core principles that underpin effective copy. Copywriting is not just about putting words on a page; it's about crafting a message that resonates with your audience and drives them to take action.

One of the key elements of copywriting is clarity. Your copy should be concise, easy to understand, and free of any confusion. You should also convey your message in a way that grabs the reader's attention and keeps them engaged.

Another fundamental aspect of copywriting is creating a unique selling proposition (USP). A USP is a distinctive feature or benefit that sets your product or service apart from the competition. By identifying and highlighting your USP, you can effectively communicate the value you offer to your target audience.

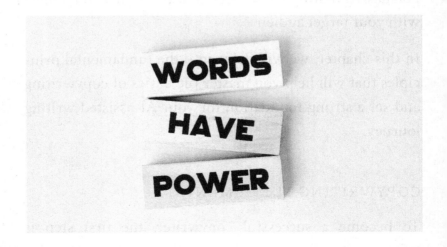

THE POWER OF PERSUASION

At the heart of copywriting lies the power of persuasion. A persuasive copy can influence readers to take a desired action, whether it's making a purchase, signing up for a newsletter, or attending an event.

When mastering the art of persuasion, it's vital to understand the psychology behind it. Utilize techniques such as social proof, scarcity, and emotional appeal to create a sense of urgency and connect with your audience on a deeper level.

CRAFTING COMPELLING HEADLINES AND HOOKS

The headline is the first impression your copy makes on your audience. It's the gatekeeper that determines whether your readers will continue reading or move on. Crafting attention-grabbing headlines is a vital skill for any copywriter.

A good headline should be compelling, concise, and relevant to your target audience's needs or desires. It should spark curiosity and entice readers to dive deeper into your copy.

Experiment with different headline formulas, such as question-based headlines, listicles, or intriguing statements, to find what resonates best with your audience.

 Create 5 headlines related to our beauty soap that we discussed above

1. "Experience Radiant Skin with Our Transformative Beauty Soap"
2. "Say Goodbye to Dull Skin: Unlock Your True Beauty with Our Beauty Soap"
3. "Discover the Secret to Glowing Skin: Introducing Our Beauty Soap"
4. "Transform Your Complexion with Our Nourishing Beauty Soap"
5. "Indulge in Luxurious Skincare: Try Our Beauty Soap for Visible Results"

A hook is another essential element of copywriting that keeps readers engaged from the beginning. It is a captivating opening line or paragraph that grabs the reader's attention and compels them to continue reading. Hooks can be thought-provoking, emotionally charged, or present a problem that the reader wants to solve.

UNDERSTANDING YOUR AUDIENCE

One of the most critical aspects of effective copywriting is understanding your audience. To create a copy that resonates with readers, you must have a deep understanding of their needs, desires, pain points, and motivations.

Research your target audience extensively to gain insights into their demographics, interests, and preferences. Conduct surveys, analyze data, and engage with your audience through social media or forums to gather valuable information. This research will help you create copy that speaks directly to your audience, addressing their concerns and providing solutions.

By understanding your audience, you can tailor your message to their specific needs, emotions, and aspirations. This level of personalization will help you build a connection and establish trust with your readers, increasing the likelihood of their taking the desired action.

3

INTRODUCTION TO CHATGPT

YOUR AI WRITING PARTNER

In the ever-evolving landscape of copywriting, technology continues to play a significant role in shaping the industry. One of the most revolutionary tools to emerge is ChatGPT, an advanced AI language model developed by OpenAI. In this chapter, we'll introduce you to ChatGPT and explore how it can become your invaluable AI writing partner.

WHAT IS CHATGPT?

ChatGPT is an AI-powered language model designed to generate human-like text based on the prompts it receives. It utilizes state-of-the-art natural language processing techniques to understand and respond to various writing tasks.

Whether you need assistance in brainstorming ideas, refining your copy, or generating engaging content, ChatGPT is there to lend a helping hand.

BENEFITS OF USING CHATGPT FOR COPYWRITING

Using ChatGPT as your AI writing partner can bring numerous benefits to your copywriting process. Let's explore some of the key advantages.

1. Enhanced Efficiency: ChatGPT can automate certain aspects of the writing process, saving you time and effort. It can assist in generating ideas, creating outlines, and refining your drafts, allowing you to focus on higher-level creative work.

2. Improved Productivity: With ChatGPT, you can amplify your productivity by harnessing its ability to generate text quickly. It can provide suggestions, rephrase sentences, and offer alternative word choices, helping you find the most effective and persuasive language.

3. Creative Inspiration: ChatGPT can be a source of creative inspiration when you're stuck or experiencing writer's block. It can generate unique ideas, provide fresh perspectives, and offer creative angles to approach your copy. With ChatGPT by your side, you'll have a constant wellspring of inspiration.

4. Language Refinement: ChatGPT can refine your copy by identifying grammar errors, suggesting improvements in style and tone, and enhancing the overall coherence of your writing. It acts as a virtual editor, ensuring that your copy is polished and professional.

GETTING STARTED WITH CHATGPT

Now that you understand the value of ChatGPT in copywriting, let's explore how you can get started with this powerful AI tool.

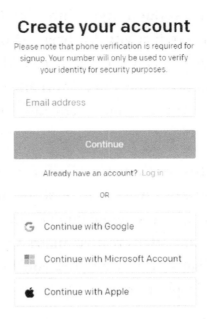

1. Sign Up and Choose a Plan: Visit the ChatGPT website and sign up for an account. Choose the plan that suits your needs, considering factors such as usage limits and pricing.

2. Familiarize Yourself with the Interface: Once you're logged in, take some time to navigate the ChatGPT interface. Familiarize yourself with the options available, such as adjusting the temperature and the maximum token limit, which can influence the output generated by the AI.

3. Crafting Effective Prompts: Providing clear and specific prompts is crucial to get the best results from ChatGPT. Clearly articulate what you need assistance with, whether it's brainstorming ideas, refining a head-line, or creating engaging introductory paragraphs.

4. Iterative Process: Remember that working with ChatGPT is iterative. The AI model may not always provide the exact output you desire on the first attempt. Refine and iterate your prompts, experiment with different approaches, and provide feedback to help train the model for better results.

5. Ethical Use and Review: While ChatGPT is a powerful tool, use it responsibly. Review and edit the output generated by ChatGPT, ensuring that it aligns with your desired goals and adheres to ethical standards. Remember, AI is a tool to augment your skills, and human judgment and oversight remain essential.

By following these steps, you can start enlisting ChatGPT as your AI writing partner. Get ready to elevate your copywriting skills, enhance your efficiency, and open up new possibilities in your creative process.

4

SETTING UP CHATGPT FOR COPYWRITING SUCCESS

To maximize the potential of ChatGPT and ensure copywriting success, it's crucial to set up the tool properly and tailor it to your specific needs.

This chapter will guide you through the process of setting up ChatGPT for optimal performance. We'll also discuss important considerations for data privacy and security.

CHOOSING THE RIGHT CHATGPT PLAN

ChatGPT offers different plans to cater to a variety of needs. When choosing the right plan for your copy-writing endeavors, consider factors such as usage limits, pricing, and access to advanced features.

Assess your usage requirements to determine the plan that aligns with your copywriting needs. If you anticipate heavy usage or have demanding projects, you might opt for a plan that offers higher usage limits. On the other hand, if your copywriting needs are more modest, a lower-tier plan may suffice.

Consider your budget as well, balancing the features and usage limits against the cost of the plan. Compare the benefits of each plan to find the one that offers the best value for your specific copywriting goals.

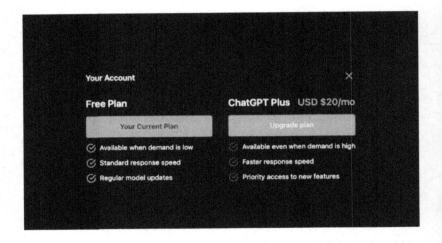

CUSTOMIZING CHATGPT TO YOUR NEEDS

Once you've chosen the right ChatGPT plan, it's time to customize the tool to enhance your copywriting experience. ChatGPT provides options for customization that allow you to tailor its output to your specific requirements.

Temperature: The temperature setting determines the randomness of the AI-generated output. Higher values (e.g., 0.8) introduce more randomness, while lower values (e.g., 0.2) result in more deterministic and focused responses. Experiment with different temperature settings to find the balance that works best for your desired output.

Max Tokens: The max tokens setting determines the length of the generated output. Setting a higher value allows for longer responses, while a lower value limits the response length. Consider the context and desired output length to set the appropriate max tokens value.

Prompting Techniques: Crafting effective prompts is key to getting the desired output from ChatGPT. Experiment with different prompting techniques to achieve the results you seek. Use clear instructions, provide examples, or guide the AI with specific criteria to generate the output you need.

Training the Model: ChatGPT benefits from user feedback and continuous improvement. As you interact with the tool, provide feedback on both positive and negative outputs. This feedback helps train the model and refine its responses over time, making them more tailored to your needs.

ENSURING DATA PRIVACY AND SECURITY

When using AI tools like ChatGPT, it's essential to prioritize data privacy and security. OpenAI takes data protection seriously and implements measures to safeguard user information.

However, it's also crucial to exercise caution and follow best practices to further protect your data. Review OpenAI's data usage and privacy policies to understand how your data is handled and stored. Familiarize yourself with the terms and conditions to comply with any data usage restrictions or guidelines.

Avoid sharing sensitive or confidential information when interacting with ChatGPT. While AI models are designed to generate responses based on the provided prompts, it's prudent to exercise caution and refrain from sharing sensitive business or personal data.

Regularly update your passwords and implement strong security practices to safeguard your ChatGPT account. Enable two-factor authentication for an extra layer of security and be vigilant against phishing attempts or suspicious activities.

With ChatGPT properly set up and customized, and data privacy and security measures in place, you're now well-prepared to fully utilize this tool for your copywriting success.

5

STRATEGIES FOR EFFECTIVE AI-ASSISTED WRITING

A I has transformed the landscape of copywriting, and with the assistance of ChatGPT, you can take your writing skills to new heights.

Now we will explore strategies for effective AI-assisted writing that will help you collaborate seamlessly with ChatGPT, speed up your writing process, generate ideas and outlines, and streamline content creation and editing.

COLLABORATING WITH CHATGPT

Collaboration is at the core of effective AI-assisted writing. ChatGPT can be your invaluable writing partner, providing inspiration, suggestions, and alternative perspectives. Here are some strategies to optimize your collaboration.

1. Prompt Iteration: Experiment with different prompts and iterate as you collaborate with ChatGPT. Refine your prompts to get the desired output and make the most of the AI's capabilities.

2. Contextual Guidance: Provide context and specific instructions in your prompts. Clearly articulate the purpose, target audience, and desired tone of the copy. The more specific your guidance, the better ChatGPT can assist you in achieving your goals.

3. Incorporating Feedback: As you interact with ChatGPT, provide feedback on its responses. Highlight what works well and areas where improvements can be made. This feedback loop helps the AI model learn and improve its future responses.

SPEEDING UP THE WRITING PROCESS

Time is of the essence in copywriting, and AI can be a game-changer in speeding up your writing process. Here are strategies to maximize your efficiency.

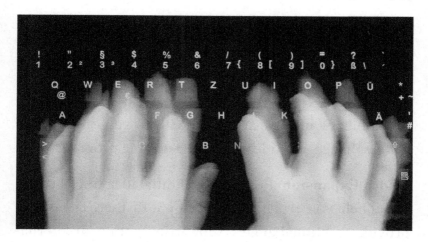

1. Automation of Routine Tasks: Delegate routine tasks to ChatGPT. It can generate boilerplate content, assist with formatting, and even proofread for grammar and style errors. By automating these tasks, you can focus on more strategic and creative aspects of copywriting.

2. Rapid Idea Generation: ChatGPT can be an invaluable resource for generating ideas quickly. Use it as an idea-generating tool to overcome writer's block or explore new angles. Leverage its creativity to brainstorm fresh concepts and perspectives.

3. Real-Time Assistance: ChatGPT's real-time responses enable you to receive immediate feedback on your writing. Use this feature to rapidly alter and refine your copy, incorporating the AI's suggestions as you go.

USING AI TO GENERATE IDEAS AND OUTLINES

Generating ideas and creating outlines are foundational steps in the copywriting process. ChatGPT can be a powerful ally in these areas. Here's how you can leverage AI to enhance your ideation and outlining process.

1. Idea Expansion: Present your initial idea to ChatGPT. It can help you expand and develop it further. The AI can provide additional angles, supporting points, or alternative approaches, enriching your concept.

2. Outlining Assistance: Use ChatGPT to generate an outline based on your initial ideas. The AI can suggest the order and structure of your content, helping you organize your thoughts and create a solid framework to build upon.

3. Incorporating AI-Generated Content: ChatGPT can generate snippets of content that you can integrate into your outline or directly into your copy. These AI-generated sections can serve as starting points or inspiration for your writing.

RO Write an outline for blog What health benefits does coffee offer?

I. Introduction
A. Hook: Captivating statement about the popularity of coffee worldwide
B. Brief overview of the topic and the health benefits of coffee
C. Thesis statement: Exploring the various health benefits that coffee offers

II. Boosts Energy and Mental Alertness
A. Explanation of how coffee stimulates the central nervous system
B. Discussion on the effects of caffeine in enhancing energy levels and mental alertness
C. Supporting evidence from scientific studies and research

III. Improves Cognitive Function
A. Explanation of how coffee enhances brain function and cognitive abilities

STREAMLINING CONTENT CREATION AND EDITING

Efficiency in content creation and editing is key to producing high-quality copy. ChatGPT can streamline these processes and help you deliver exceptional content.

Consider the following strategies.

1. Content Expansion: When you have a rough draft, leverage ChatGPT to expand and enrich your content. Use the AI's language generation capabilities to add depth, supporting details, and persuasive language to your copy.

2. Language Enhancement: ChatGPT can help you refine the style, tone, and clarity of your writing. Present your copy to the AI for suggestions on sentence structure, vocabulary choice, and overall coherence. It can go a long way to polish your copy for maximum impact.

3. Editing Support: Utilize ChatGPT as a virtual editor. It can spot grammar and spelling errors, suggest improvements, and ensure consistency throughout your copy. Collaborating with the AI in the editing phase helps you produce error-free and professional content.

By implementing these strategies, you can effectively collaborate with ChatGPT, expedite your writing process, leverage AI-generated ideas and outlines, and streamline content creation and editing.

The power of AI-assisted writing is at your fingertips, allowing you to produce high-quality copy efficiently and with enhanced creativity.

6

PERFECTING YOUR CRAFT

ENHANCING SKILLS WITH CHATGPT

Constantly honing your copywriting skills is essential for staying ahead in the industry's competitive landscape. ChatGPT can be your secret weapon for perfecting your craft and taking your writing to the next level.

This chapter will cover how you can leverage ChatGPT to enhance your grammar and style, improve clarity and readability, incorporate emotional appeal, and unleash your creativity.

LEVERAGING CHATGPT FOR GRAMMAR AND STYLE

Effective copywriting requires impeccable grammar and a polished writing style. ChatGPT can be a valuable tool to help you refine your grammar and style, ensuring your copy is professional and error-free.

When collaborating with ChatGPT, pay attention to the suggestions it provides for sentence structure, word choice, and grammar improvements. Use its expertise to enhance the flow of your writing and eliminate any grammatical errors. By incorporating AI's suggestions, you'll elevate the quality of your copy and create a more enjoyable reading experience for your audience.

IMPROVING CLARITY AND READABILITY

Clarity and readability are paramount in copywriting. Your message should be crystal-clear and easily comprehensible to your target audience. ChatGPT can help maximize the clarity and readability of your copy.

When working with ChatGPT, consider the following strategies.

1. Simplify Complex Concepts: If you're dealing with complex or technical subject matter, present it to ChatGPT and seek its assistance in simplifying the language. The AI can help you translate intricate ideas into more accessible terms, ensuring your copy is understood by a wider audience. See this example of simplified Newton's second law for fifth graders:

Hey there, let's talk about Newton's first law of motion. It's a cool law that tells us how objects behave when all the forces acting on them are balanced.

Okay, imagine you're playing with a toy car on a flat surface. If you don't push or pull the car, it will just stay still, right? That's because the forces acting on it are balanced. We call this "equilibrium."

Now, if you want the car to start moving, you need to give it a little push or pull. This creates an unbalanced force, and the car will start accelerating. Acceleration means the car will either speed up, change direction, or even both!

But here's the catch: if the forces acting on the car become balanced again, it will go back to its original state of rest or keep moving at a steady speed.

So, remember, according to Newton's first law, if the forces are balanced, there is no acceleration. But if there's an unbalanced force, then things start to get interesting!

2. Check for Coherence: ChatGPT can help you identify and resolve any coherence issues in your copy. It can suggest transitional phrases, logical connectors, and improved sentence structures to improve the flow of your writing.

3. Enhance Paragraph Structure: If your paragraphs seem disjointed or lack cohesion, collaborate with ChatGPT to streamline their structure. The AI can provide suggestions on improving paragraph transitions, maintaining a logical progression of ideas, and creating a smoother reading experience.

INCORPORATING EMOTIONAL APPEAL

Copywriting is not just about conveying information; it's about evoking emotions in your audience. Emotional appeal can captivate readers and drive them to take action. ChatGPT can be a valuable resource in infusing your copy with emotional resonance.

When collaborating with ChatGPT, consider the following techniques.

1. Tone and Language: Experiment with different tones and language styles to evoke specific emotions. ChatGPT can suggest persuasive and emotive language that resonates with your target audience.

 Rewrite following text in Casual tone for beginners:

The new subscription plan, ChatGPT Plus, will be available for $20/month, and subscribers will receive a number of benefits:

General access to ChatGPT, even during peak times
Faster response times
Priority access to new features and improvements
ChatGPT Plus is available to customers in the United States and around the world.A
[A]
We expanded access to ChatGPT Plus for customers outside of the United States on February 10th, 2023.

2. Storytelling: ChatGPT can assist you in crafting compelling narratives and stories that draw out emotions. Present the core elements of your story to the AI and work with it to refine the plot, characters, and emotional arcs.

3. Use of Imagery and Metaphors: Collaborate with ChatGPT to find unique and impactful imagery or metaphors that enhance the emotional impact of your copy. The AI can generate descriptive language or offer creative suggestions to bring your copy to life.

ENHANCING CREATIVITY WITH AI

Creativity is the lifeblood of copywriting. ChatGPT can act as a catalyst for unleashing your creative potential, offering fresh perspectives, and inspiring innovative ideas.

Consider the following strategies to enhance your creativity with ChatGPT.

1. Brainstorming Sessions: Use ChatGPT as a virtual brainstorming partner. Engage in free-flowing conversations with the AI, bouncing ideas back and forth to stimulate your creativity. Let the AI generate novel concepts, unexpected angles, or unique approaches to fuel your creative process.

2. Prompt Exploration: Experiment with different types of prompts to unlock new creative avenues. Present open-ended questions, hypothetical scenarios, or challenging prompts to inspire out-of-the-box thinking. Collaborate with ChatGPT to explore unconventional ideas and push the boundaries of your copywriting.

3. Embrace Serendipity: Sometimes, AI-generated responses may surprise you with unexpected brilliance.

Embrace these serendipitous moments and be open to incorporating them into your copy. ChatGPT can provide a new perspective that sparks your creative genius.

By leveraging ChatGPT to enhance your grammar and style, improve clarity and readability, incorporate emotional appeal, and unleash your creativity, you'll make significant strides in perfecting your copywriting.

7

WRITING ADVERTISEMENTS WITH CHATGPT

Advertising is a critical component of copywriting. With the power of ChatGPT, you can create impactful and persuasive ad copy that drives conversions.

We'll now explore strategies for crafting high-converting ad copy, creating influential sales pages, and optimizing ad performance with the assistance of AI.

CRAFTING HIGH-CONVERTING AD COPY

Writing ad copy that captures attention, generates interest, and compels action is an art form. ChatGPT can be a valuable tool in your arsenal as you craft high-converting ad copy.

Consider the following strategies.

1. Captivating Headlines: Begin with a headline that grabs the reader's attention and piques their curiosity. Collaborate with ChatGPT to generate attention-grabbing headlines that resonate with your target audience.

 Write attention-grabbing headlines

Product: Copy Beauty Soap
Target Audience: Women aged 25-45 who prioritize skincare and seek high-quality beauty products.
Goal: Increase brand awareness, drive traffic to the website, and generate product sales.

Key Messaging Points:

Unique Selling Proposition: Highlight the key features and benefits that differentiate the beauty soap from competitors.

1. "Discover the Secret to Flawless Skin: Experience the Power of Copy Beauty Soap!"
2. "Unlock Your Skin's Potential: Reveal Radiance with Copy Beauty Soap!"
3. "The Beauty Breakthrough You've Been Waiting For: Copy Beauty Soap - Transform Your Skin Today!"

2. Clear Value Proposition: Clearly communicate the unique value and benefits your product or service offers. Use ChatGPT to refine your value proposition and convey it in a concise and engaging manner.

3. Emotional Appeal: Infuse your ad copy with an emotional appeal to establish a connection with your audience. Collaborate with ChatGPT to evoke specific emotions that resonate with your target audience and drive them to take action.

CREATING PERSUASIVE SALES PAGES

A persuasive sales page can make all the difference in converting potential customers into paying customers. ChatGPT can assist you in creating persuasive sales pages that engage and convince your audience.

Consider the following strategies.

1. Compelling Opening: Use ChatGPT to craft an opening that immediately captures the reader's attention and conveys the value and benefits they'll gain from your product or service. Use persuasive language and collaborate with the AI to refine the opening for maximum impact.

2. Highlighting Features and Benefits: Employ ChatGPT to showcase your product or service's key features and benefits. The AI can help you articulate them in a way that resonates with your target audience and highlights their value.

3. Overcoming Objections: Anticipate potential objections your audience may have and address them on your sales page. Use ChatGPT to provide compelling responses to these objections, addressing concerns and building trust.

OPTIMIZING AD PERFORMANCE WITH AI

AI can be a game-changer in optimizing ad performance. ChatGPT can provide valuable insights and suggestions to enhance your ad campaigns and maximize their effectiveness.

Consider the following strategies.

1. Ad Copy Testing: Employ ChatGPT to generate multiple variations of your ad copy. A/B tests these variations to determine the most effective messaging, tone, and language. Use the AI's suggestions to refine and improve your ad copy for better performance. Here's an example of generating two versions of the same ad for A/B testing.

Version A:

"Experience the Ultimate Skin Transformation with Copy Beauty Soap. Our unique formula, enriched with natural ingredients, deeply cleanses, brightens, and nourishes your skin. Say hello to a radiant, flawless complexion. Try Copy Beauty Soap today and unleash your skin's true beauty!"

Version B:

"Unlock Your Skin's Potential with Copy Beauty Soap. Our luxurious soap is specifically designed to rejuvenate and revitalize your skin. Experience the power of natural ingredients that deeply cleanse, hydrate, and restore your skin's radiance. Elevate your skincare routine with Copy Beauty Soap and discover the confidence that comes with healthy, glowing skin!"

2. Ad Targeting: Leverage ChatGPT's capabilities to identify and refine your target audience. Utilize AI to generate insights on audience demographics, interests, and preferences. Use these insights to optimize your ad targeting and increase the relevance of your messaging.

3. Performance Monitoring: Monitor the performance of your ad campaigns and collaborate with ChatGPT to analyze the data. The AI can help identify trends, patterns, and areas for improvement. Utilize its insights to make data-driven decisions and optimize your ad performance.

By leveraging ChatGPT to craft high-converting ad copy, create persuasive sales pages, and optimize ad performance, you can create gripping advertisements that drive results.

8

USING CHATGPT FOR CONTENT MARKETING

C ontent marketing is a powerful strategy for building brand awareness, driving traffic, and engaging your target audience. With the assistance of ChatGPT, you can elevate your content marketing efforts to new heights.

In this chapter, we'll explore how you can use ChatGPT to create captivating blog posts, craft informative articles, develop shareable infographics, and generate viral content ideas.

CREATING CAPTIVATING BLOG POSTS

Blog posts are a cornerstone of content marketing, providing a platform to educate, entertain, and engage your audience. ChatGPT can be a valuable resource as you create captivating blog posts.

Consider the following strategies.

1. Engaging Introductions: Utilize ChatGPT to craft compelling introductions that hook your readers from the start. Experiment with different opening lines or questions, and refine them with the AI's suggestions to draw your audience's attention.

2. Storytelling Elements: Humans are naturally drawn to stories. Employ ChatGPT to incorporate storytelling elements into your blog posts. The AI can help you develop narratives, create relatable characters, and weave compelling stories that resonate with your readers.

> I want to write a blog post about Coffee health benefits. Follow storytelling style for this. Create a character name Linda who is a Coffeeholic and tell her story and feelings about coffe while describing the health benefits.

> Title: Linda's Journey: How Coffee Became Her Healthful Addiction
>
> Introduction:
> Meet Linda, a vivacious and passionate coffee lover. For Linda, coffee isn't just a beverage; it's a beloved companion that has accompanied her on life's journey. In this blog post, we'll dive into Linda's story and explore the fascinating health benefits she has discovered along the way. From boosting energy levels to enhancing mental focus, join Linda as she unravels the secrets behind her favorite indulgence.

3. Providing Actionable Insights: Use ChatGPT to provide valuable, actionable insights in your blog posts.

The AI can help you generate practical tips, expert advice, or step-by-step instructions that empower your audience to take action and derive real value from your content.

CRAFTING INFORMATIVE ARTICLES

Informative articles establish your authority in your industry and provide valuable knowledge to your target audience. ChatGPT can assist you in crafting informative articles that educate and engage your readers.

Consider the following strategies.

1. Research Assistance: Utilize ChatGPT to gather relevant information and research material for your articles. The AI can help you explore various sources, generate data-backed insights, and provide a well-rounded perspective on the topic.

2. Structuring the Content: Use ChatGPT to outline and structure your article effectively. Utilize the AI to create logical sections, headings, and subheadings that guide your readers through the content and ensure clarity and coherence.

3. Explaining Complex Concepts: Utilize ChatGPT to simplify complex concepts and explain them in a clear and accessible manner. The AI can help you break down intricate ideas, provide examples, and use analogies to enhance your readers' understanding.

DEVELOPING SHAREABLE INFOGRAPHICS

Infographics are visually appealing and highly shareable, making them an excellent asset for content marketing. ChatGPT can assist you in developing informative and visually striking infographics.

Consider the following strategies.

1. Data Presentation: Collaborate with ChatGPT to present data in a visually compelling way. The AI can help you identify key data points, generate charts or graphs, and suggest impactful ways to present information.

2. Storytelling with Visuals: Infographics can tell a story through visuals. Employ ChatGPT to create a visual narrative that guides your audience through the information. The AI can suggest visual elements, icons, or illustrations to enhance the storytelling aspect of your infographic.

3. Sharing Valuable Insights: Employ ChatGPT to ensure your infographic conveys valuable insights. The

AI can help you generate concise, impactful text that complements the visual elements and provides actionable takeaways for your audience.

GENERATING VIRAL CONTENT IDEAS

Viral content has the power to generate significant attention and engagement. ChatGPT can assist you in generating viral content ideas that resonate with your audience and capture their attention.

Consider the following strategies.

1. Trend Analysis: Utilize ChatGPT to analyze current trends and identify topics or themes that have the potential to go viral. The AI can help you understand what's capturing the interest of your audience and suggest creative angles to capitalize on those trends.

2. Unique Perspectives: Collaborate with ChatGPT to generate unique perspectives or alternative viewpoints on popular topics. The AI's creativity can inspire fresh ideas that stand out in a crowded content landscape, increasing the likelihood of your content going viral.

3. Emotional Appeal: Enlist ChatGPT to infuse emotional appeal into your content ideas. The AI can help you generate ideas that evoke strong emotions, such as humor, surprise, or inspiration, increasing the share-ability and virality of your content.

Example of generating humorous video titles that can go viral:

 Write some humorous video titles related to Coffee that people will love

1. "Confessions of a Coffee Addict: How Many Cups is Too Many?"
2. "The Coffee Chronicles: Adventures of a Caffeine Junkie"
3. "The Coffee Challenge: Can You Handle the Caffeine?"
4. "Coffee: The Ultimate Superpower in a Mug"
5. "Coffee 101: How to Speak Fluent Caffeine"
6. "Coffee Lovers Unite: The Great Bean Debate"
7. "The Coffee Olympics: Who Brews the Best Cup?"
8. "Coffee Hacks: How to Survive Mornings Without Spilling a Drop"
9. "The Coffee Detective: Solving the Mystery of the Perfect Brew"
10. "Coffee Therapy: Curing the Grumpy Mornings, One Sip at a Time"

EMAIL MARKETING

LEVERAGING AI FOR ENGAGING CONTENT

E mail marketing remains a powerful strategy for engaging with your audience, nurturing leads, and driving conversions. With the assistance of AI, specifically ChatGPT, you can take your email marketing efforts to new heights.

Let's explore how you can leverage AI to write effective email copy, personalize email campaigns, conduct A/B testing and optimization, and maximize open and click-through rates.

WRITING EFFECTIVE EMAIL COPY

The success of your email marketing campaigns hinges on the quality of your email copy. Compelling and persuasive email copy captures attention, entices readers, and motivates them to take action. With the assistance of ChatGPT, you can craft email copy that drives results.

Consider the following strategies.

1. Attention-Grabbing Subject Lines: Collaborate with ChatGPT to generate attention-grabbing subject lines that compel recipients to open your emails. Experiment with different subject line variations, incorporating persuasive language or personalized elements to pique curiosity and interest.

 Write some Attention-Grabbing Email Subject Lines related to Coffee that people will surely open

1. "Wake Up and Smell the Coffee! Exclusive Offers Inside"
2. "Your Daily Dose of Coffee Magic Awaits"
3. "Attention Coffee Lovers: This Is Not a Drill"
4. "Revive Your Morning Routine with Our Special Coffee Surprise"
5. "Sip, Savor, Repeat: Discover Our Irresistible Coffee Collection"
6. "Don't Miss Out on the Ultimate Coffee Experience"
7. "Coffee Break Alert: Unveiling Our New Flavors"
8. "Get Your Coffee Fix: Limited-Time Offer Inside"
9. "Fuel Your Day with the Perfect Cup of Coffee"
10. "Unlock the Secrets of Coffee Bliss: Exclusive Insider Access"

2. Concise and Compelling Content: Utilize ChatGPT to help you refine your messaging, choose persuasive language, and structure your emails in a way that maintains the reader's interest and leads them smoothly toward the desired action.

3. Call-to-Action Optimization: Use ChatGPT to optimize your call-to-action (CTA) statements. The AI can assist you in crafting clear and persuasive CTAs that prompt readers to take a desired action, whether it's making a purchase, signing up for a webinar, or downloading a resource.

PERSONALIZING EMAIL CAMPAIGNS WITH AI

Personalization is key to building strong relationships with your audience and increasing engagement. ChatGPT can assist you in personalizing your email campaigns to create a more tailored and relevant experience for each recipient.

Consider the following strategies.

1. Dynamic Content Generation: Use ChatGPT to generate dynamic content that is personalized to each recipient. The AI can help you incorporate recipient-specific details, such as their name, location, or previous interactions, to create a more personalized and engaging email experience.

2. Segmentation Assistance: Utilize ChatGPT to segment your email list effectively. The AI can analyze audience data, identify common characteristics or behaviors, and suggest segmentation strategies that allow you to send more targeted and personalized emails to specific groups.

3. Behavioral Triggers: Collaborate with ChatGPT to identify behavioral triggers that can automate personalized email campaigns. The AI can help you set up triggers based on actions or events, such as abandoned carts, recent purchases, or specific website interactions, ensuring that each recipient receives relevant and timely emails.

A/B TESTING AND OPTIMIZATION

A/B testing is a crucial part of optimizing your email marketing campaigns. With the assistance of ChatGPT, you can conduct effective A/B tests and optimize your emails for better performance.

Consider the following strategies.

1. Test Variables: Use ChatGPT to identify variables that you can test in your email campaigns. These variables could include subject lines, email content, CTAs, or visual elements. The AI can suggest variations and help set up A/B tests to determine the most effective options.

2. Analyze Results: Utilize ChatGPT to analyze the results of your A/B tests. The AI can help you interpret the data, identify patterns or trends, and provide insights on which variations perform better. Use these insights to optimize your future email campaigns.

MAXIMIZING OPEN AND CLICK-THROUGH RATES

The success of your email marketing campaigns relies heavily on open and click-through rates. ChatGPT can assist you in maximizing these rates through various strategies.

Consider the following approaches.

1. Subject Line Optimization: Collaborate with ChatGPT to optimize your subject lines for maximum open rates. Experiment with variations by incorporating personalization or urgency, then refine them with the AI's suggestions.

2. Compelling Preheaders: Use ChatGPT to create winning preheaders that complement your subject lines and entice recipients to open your emails. The AI can help you generate short, attention-grabbing text that provides a glimpse of what's inside, increasing the chances of engagement.

 Write email preheaders for email with subject line "Wake Up and Smell the Coffee! Exclusive Offers Inside"

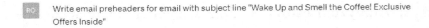

1. "Discover the Aroma and Taste of Premium Coffee in Our Exclusive Offers"
2. "Start Your Day Right with Exclusive Coffee Offers You Won't Want to Miss"
3. "Indulge in the Rich Flavor and Savings of Our Exclusive Coffee Deals"
4. "Unveiling Exclusive Coffee Offers: Wake Up to Irresistible Savings"
5. "Experience Coffee Perfection with Our Exclusive Offers and Discounts"
6. "Get Ready to Savor Every Sip: Exclusive Coffee Offers Await You"
7. "Your Morning Just Got Better: Exclusive Offers on Your Favorite Coffee"

3. Clear and Persuasive CTAs: Collaborate with ChatGPT to optimize your CTAs for higher click-through rates. The AI can help you craft clear, persuasive, and action-oriented CTAs that prompt recipients to click and take the desired action.

By leveraging AI, particularly ChatGPT, for email marketing, you can write effective email copy, personalize email campaigns, conduct A/B testing and optimization, and maximize open and click-through rates.

10

SEO COPYWRITING WITH CHATGPT

GETTING YOUR CONTENT SEEN

In today's digital landscape, search engine optimization (SEO) plays a vital role in getting your content discovered by your target audience. With the assistance of ChatGPT, you can optimize your copywriting for search engines and increase your visibility.

Now we'll explore the principles of SEO copywriting, strategies for optimizing content, generating SEO-friendly meta tags, and researching and incorporating keywords effectively.

UNDERSTANDING SEO PRINCIPLES

To excel in SEO copywriting, understanding search engine optimization is crucial.

Here are fundamental principles to keep in mind.

1. Relevance: Search engines aim to deliver the most relevant results to users. Your content should align with the intent and interests of your target audience, providing valuable information or solving their problems.

2. Authority: Search engines value authoritative content. Establishing your expertise, credibility, and trustworthiness through well-researched, accurate, and comprehensive content can boost your visibility in search results.

> RO   I want to be an authority in Coffee maker niche. Which Silo structure should I follow for SEO?

> To establish yourself as an authority in the coffee maker niche and optimize your website for SEO, you can follow a silo structure that organizes your content into specific categories related to coffee makers. Here's a suggested silo structure:
>
> 1. Main Category: Coffee Makers
>   * Subcategory 1: Drip Coffee Makers
>   * Subcategory 2: Espresso Machines
>   * Subcategory 3: Single Serve Coffee Makers
>   * Subcategory 4: French Presses
>   * Subcategory 5: Pour-Over Coffee Makers

3. User Experience: User experience is paramount. Ensure your content is user-friendly, easily navigable, and optimized for different devices. A positive user experience enhances engagement and encourages users to spend more time on your site.

OPTIMIZING CONTENT FOR SEARCH ENGINES

Optimizing your content for search engines involves several strategies and techniques. Collaborating with ChatGPT can help you implement effective optimization methods.

Consider the following strategies.

1. Compelling Titles: Use ChatGPT to create enticing and keyword-rich titles for your content. The AI can help you generate attention-grabbing titles that reflect the content's focus and incorporate relevant keywords.

 Write some SEO friendly title for a blog post about Best Coffee Makers in 2023

 "Top Coffee Makers of 2023: The Ultimate Guide for Coffee Lovers"

"The Best Coffee Makers in 2023: Discover Your Perfect Brew"

"2023's Top-Rated Coffee Makers: Elevate Your Morning Routine"

"Coffee Lovers Rejoice: The Best Coffee Makers to Own in 2023"

"Find Your Perfect Cup: The Best Coffee Makers of 2023 Revealed"

"Upgrade Your Morning Ritual: The Best Coffee Makers for 2023"

"2023's Must-Have Coffee Makers: Brew Your Way to Perfection"

2. Well-Structured Headings: Work with ChatGPT to structure your content with clear and hierarchical headings. Utilize heading tags (H1, H2, etc.) effectively, ensuring they align with the content's organization and include relevant keywords where appropriate.

3. Engaging Content: Utilize ChatGPT to create engaging, informative, and valuable content that resonates with your audience. The AI can refine your messaging, provide insights, and assist in organizing your content to make it more readable.

RO   Write an Engaging Intro Content about best coffee makers.

Introduction:

Calling all coffee enthusiasts and connoisseurs! If you're on a quest for the perfect cup of joe, you've come to the right place. In a world filled with countless options, finding the best coffee maker can feel like navigating through a dense jungle of features, styles, and brewing methods. But fear not, as we're here to be your guiding light on this aromatic journey.

Picture waking up to the enticing aroma of freshly brewed coffee, as the rich and bold flavors dance on your taste buds. Whether you prefer the simplicity of a classic drip coffee maker, the artistry of an espresso machine, or the convenience of a single-serve brewer, our mission is to help you discover the coffee maker that will transform your morning routine into a daily ritual of pure bliss.

GENERATING SEO-FRIENDLY META TAGS

Meta tags are HTML tags that provide information about your web page to search engines. Optimizing these tags can enhance your SEO efforts. Use ChatGPT to generate SEO-friendly meta tags for your content.

Consider the following strategies.

RO · Write meta title, description and image Alt text for 2023's Top-Rated Coffee Makers: Elevate Your Morning Routine

Meta Title: "2023's Top-Rated Coffee Makers: Elevate Your Morning Routine"

Meta Description: Discover the best coffee makers of 2023 to enhance your morning routine. From drip coffee makers to espresso machines, explore our curated selection of top-rated models that deliver exceptional brewing performance and elevate your coffee experience.

Image Alt Text: "2023's Top-Rated Coffee Makers: Elevate Your Morning Routine - Image of coffee maker with freshly brewed cup of coffee"

Note: The image Alt text should be descriptive of the image content and include relevant keywords.

1. Title Tags: Use ChatGPT to generate compelling and keyword-rich title tags that accurately describe your content. The AI can help you craft succinct and enticing title tags that catch the attention of search engine users.

2. Meta Descriptions: Collaborate with ChatGPT to create informative and persuasive meta descriptions. These descriptions should summarize the content's key points, incorporate relevant keywords, and encourage users to click on your search result.

3. Image Alt Text: Utilize ChatGPT to generate descriptive alt text for your images. Alt text not only enhances accessibility but also provides an opportunity to include relevant keywords. The AI can assist in generating alt text that accurately describes the image and aligns with your content's focus.

RESEARCHING AND INCORPORATING KEYWORDS

Keywords are essential elements in SEO copywriting, as they help search engines understand the relevance of your content.

Collaborating with ChatGPT can streamline your keyword research process and assist in incorporating them effectively.

Consider the following strategies.

1. Keyword Research: Work with ChatGPT to conduct keyword research and identify relevant keywords for your content. The AI can suggest popular and highly searched terms, provide insights on keyword competition, and help you target long-tail keywords specific to your niche.

2. Natural Integration: Use ChatGPT to naturally integrate keywords into your content. The AI can help you seamlessly incorporate keywords into your copy, ensuring they fit naturally and don't disrupt the flow of your writing. This natural integration allows search engines to recognize the relevance of your content without compromising its readability and user experience.

Example of natural integration of keywords:

 Calling all coffee enthusiasts and connoisseurs! If you're on a quest for the perfect cup of joe, you've come to the right place. In a world filled with countless options, finding the best coffee maker can feel like navigating through a dense jungle of features, styles, and brewing methods. But fear not, as we're here to be your guiding light on this aromatic journey.

Picture waking up to the enticing aroma of freshly brewed coffee, as the rich and bold flavors dance on your taste buds. Whether you prefer the simplicity of a classic drip coffee maker, the artistry of an espresso machine, or the convenience of a single-serve brewer, our mission is to help you discover the best coffee maker that will transform your morning routine into a daily ritual of pure bliss. With our comprehensive reviews and expert recommendations, you can confidently navigate the vast landscape of coffee makers and find the one that suits your taste preferences and lifestyle.

3. Keyword Placement: Utilize ChatGPT to strategically place keywords in key areas of your content. These areas include the title, headings, subheadings, introductory and concluding paragraphs, and throughout the body of the text.

The AI can provide suggestions on keyword placement to maximize their impact and improve your content's visibility in search results.

4. Long-Tail Keywords: Collaborate with ChatGPT to identify and utilize long-tail keywords. Long-tail keywords are more specific phrases that target niche topics or user intents. Incorporating long-tail keywords can help you reach a more targeted audience and compete in less saturated search results.

 Suggest some long tail keywords related to coffee makers

1. "Best coffee maker for home use"
2. "Top-rated espresso machine for beginners"
3. "Affordable drip coffee maker with programmable timer"
4. "Single-serve coffee maker with reusable pods"
5. "Coffee maker with built-in grinder and frother"
6. "High-capacity coffee maker for large households"
7. "Stylish and compact coffee maker for small spaces"
8. "Best budget-friendly coffee maker under $100"
9. "Versatile coffee maker for both ground coffee and pods

5. Monitoring and Optimization: Work with ChatGPT to monitor the performance of your SEO efforts. The AI can assist you in analyzing data, such as search rankings, organic traffic, and user engagement metrics.

Evaluating these insights helps you identify areas for improvement, refine your content strategy, and continuously optimize your copy for better SEO results.

By understanding and implementing SEO principles, optimizing your content for search engines, generating

SEO-friendly meta tags, and researching and incorporating keywords effectively with the assistance of ChatGPT, you can significantly enhance the visibility of your content and attract organic traffic.

MAKING AI PART OF THE CONVERSATION

"Some people call this artificial intelligence, but the reality is this technology will enhance us."

— GINNI ROMETTY

We discussed the fear of automation in Chapter 1, and if you picked up this book with some skepticism, that's completely understandable. Anyone who works with words knows that it requires craftsmanship, and the idea of signing that creativity over to AI is a terrifying thought for many writers.

Hopefully, by now, your fears have subsided, and you're starting to see how AI can be a useful tool that allows you to focus on those high-level creative jobs while helping you with the more mundane, repetitive tasks.

In a sense, it's like having a personal assistant who can take care of your administrative tasks while you focus on the more satisfying parts of your job. Since it's here to stay, I think it's essential for copywriters to understand how to use it to their advantage.

I want to get this understanding out to as many copywriters as possible. Not only will this help them individually, but it will help to prevent fragmentation in the community – if AI is a consistent part of the conversation, everyone will know they're on the same page, and pooling skills and resources will become a much simpler job.

Unfortunately, this isn't a task I can farm out to AI just yet, so I'd like to ask for your help.

By leaving a review of this book on Amazon, you'll show your fellow copywriters where they can find exactly what they need to know about AI to use it to their best advantage in their work.

Simply by telling new readers how this book has helped you and what they can expect to find inside, you'll let them know that there's nothing to fear and that AI has great potential in their line of work.

Thank you for your support. AI is here to stay – let's ensure everyone knows how to use it.

11

SOCIAL MEDIA COPYWRITING

FAST, CONSISTENT, ENGAGING

Social media platforms have revolutionized the way businesses connect with their audience. To thrive in the competitive social media landscape, it's crucial to master the art of social media copywriting. By enlisting AI, specifically ChatGPT, you can create fast, consistent, and engaging social media posts that captivate your audience.

We will now explore strategies for crafting engaging social media posts, leveraging AI for social media copy, scheduling and analyzing social media content, and maximizing reach and engagement.

CRAFTING ENGAGING SOCIAL MEDIA POSTS

Crafting engaging social media posts requires a blend of creativity, concise messaging, and a deep understanding of your audience. Collaborate with ChatGPT to create posts that capture attention and inspire action.

Consider the following strategies.

1. Compelling Hooks: Utilize ChatGPT to generate compelling hooks that grab your audience's attention within the first few seconds. The AI can assist you in crafting intriguing openings, asking thought-provoking questions, or sharing surprising facts that entice users to read further.

2. Concise Messaging: Social media platforms have limited space for text. Employ ChatGPT to refine your messaging, ensuring it is concise, impactful, and aligned with your brand voice. The AI can help you distill your message into bite-sized content that resonates with your audience.

3. Visual Appeal: Visuals play a crucial role in social media engagement. Collaborate with ChatGPT to identify eye-catching visuals or generate compelling captions that enhance the impact of your posts. The AI can assist in providing descriptive and engaging text to accompany your images or videos.

LEVERAGING AI FOR SOCIAL MEDIA COPY

AI can be a valuable asset in streamlining your social media copywriting process. Use ChatGPT to leverage its capabilities and enhance your social media presence.

Consider the following approaches.

1. Generating Ideas: Work with ChatGPT to generate ideas for your social media posts. The AI can provide inspiration, suggest trending topics, or help you brainstorm unique angles to engage your audience.

2. Language Enhancement: Collaborate with ChatGPT to enhance your social media copy with persuasive language and compelling phrases. The AI can assist in refining your messaging, offering alternative word choices, and ensuring your posts resonate with your audience.

3. Brand Consistency: Maintaining a consistent brand voice across social media platforms is a must. Use ChatGPT to ensure your social media copy aligns with your brand guidelines. The AI can help you maintain consistency in tone, language, and messaging to reinforce your brand identity.

SCHEDULING AND ANALYZING SOCIAL MEDIA CONTENT

To maintain a consistent social media presence, plan and schedule your content effectively. Utilize ChatGPT to optimize your social media scheduling and analyze the performance of your posts.

Consider the following strategies.

1. Content Calendar: ChatGPT can create a content calendar that outlines your social media posts in advance. You can also use the AI to organize your content, identify the best times to post, and maintain a consistent publishing schedule.

 Make a social media content calendar for my Coffee shop

 Social Media Content Calendar for [Coffee Shop Name]

Month: [Month]

Week 1:

- Monday: Start the week with a fun coffee fact and an enticing photo of your specialty coffee blend.
- Wednesday: Share a customer testimonial or review highlighting their favorite drink and experience at your coffee shop.
- Friday: Feature a behind-the-scenes video of your baristas crafting latte art or preparing a unique coffee recipe.

2. Post Optimization: Use ChatGPT to optimize your social media posts for maximum impact. The AI can suggest optimal post lengths, ideal hashtags, and engaging call-to-action statements to encourage audience interaction.

3. Performance Analysis: Utilize ChatGPT to analyze the performance of your social media content. The AI can help you track key metrics, such as reach, engagement, click-through rates, and conversions. By evaluating these insights, you can refine your social media strategy and improve future content performance.

MAXIMIZING REACH AND ENGAGEMENT

Maximizing reach and engagement on social media requires a strategic approach. Employ ChatGPT to implement effective tactics that boost your social media presence.

Consider the following approaches.

1. Influencer Collaboration: Make use of ChatGPT to identify potential influencers or industry experts to collaborate with. The AI can help you research and connect with relevant influencers, leveraging their audience to expand your reach and increase engagement. Consider the following example of a short message to collaborate with an Instagram influencer:

Subject: Collaboration Opportunity: Coffee Shop x Influencer

Hi [Influencer's Name],

I love your coffee content! Let's collaborate and bring your coffee passion to our coffee shop. Interested?

Best,
[Your Name]
[Your Coffee Shop Name]
[Contact Information]

2. User-Generated Content: Utilize ChatGPT to encourage user-generated content. The AI can assist in creating prompts or contests that inspire your audience to create and share content related to your brand. This content not only boosts engagement but also generates authentic user testimonials and brand advocacy.

3. Trend Monitoring: Use ChatGPT to monitor social media trends and capitalize on relevant topics or hashtags. The AI can help you identify trending conversations, enabling you to participate in timely discussions and increase your visibility within your target audience.

12

VIDEO SALES LETTERS

USING CHATGPT TO CREATE ENGAGING VISUAL NARRATIVES

Video sales letters (VSLs) have emerged as a highly effective tool for captivating audiences and driving conversions. In this chapter, we'll explore how ChatGPT can create compelling VSLs that leave a lasting impact on viewers.

By harnessing the power of AI, you can enhance your storytelling abilities, create visually stunning narratives, and optimize your VSLs for maximum engagement and conversion.

1. Understanding the Power of VSLs: Dive into the world of VSLs and their immense potential to capture an audience's attention. Explore why they are a vital component of any successful marketing campaign and how they can effectively convey your message.

2. Collaborating with ChatGPT: Learn how to harness the power of ChatGPT as your AI writing partner for VSLs. Discover how AI-generated suggestions and insights can assist you in crafting a compelling script that aligns with your marketing objectives.

3. Crafting a Captivating VSL Script: Discover the step-by-step process of collaborating with ChatGPT to create a persuasive VSL script. Learn how to identify your target audience, address their pain points, highlight the benefits of your product or service, and create a compelling call to action.

4. Enhancing Visual Appeal: Explore the role of visuals in VSLs and how they can significantly impact viewer engagement. Learn how to work with ChatGPT to incorporate visually stunning graphics, animations, and transitions that support your script and captivate your audience.

5. Optimizing VSL Performance: Understand the importance of testing and optimizing your VSLs to maximize their effectiveness. Explore how ChatGPT can assist in analyzing viewer engagement, identifying areas for improvement, and iterating on your VSLs to enhance their conversion rates.

6. Harnessing AI for Voiceover and Subtitles: Discover how ChatGPT can aid in generating high-quality voiceover scripts and subtitles for your VSLs. Explore the potential of AI in creating multilingual VSLs and reaching a broader audience.

> RO   Write a NAS Daily style Video script for a video about health benefits of coffee

> [Opening Shot: Vibrant coffee shop ambiance with people enjoying their cups of coffee]
>
> Narrator: "Hey there! Welcome to today's episode of 'Coffee Chronicles.' Today, we're diving into the wonderful world of coffee and uncovering its amazing health benefits. So grab your favorite cup of joe, sit back, and let's get started!"
>
> [Cut to shots of coffee being brewed, poured, and enjoyed]
>
> Narrator: "Coffee has been enjoyed by cultures around the world for centuries, and it's more than just a morning pick-me-up. Did you know that coffee offers a plethora of health benefits? Let's explore some of the remarkable ways coffee can positively impact our well-being."

7. Integrating Music and Sound Effects: Learn how to collaborate with ChatGPT to select suitable music tracks and sound effects that enhance the emotional impact of your VSLs. Understand the role of AI in helping you find copyright-free music and create the perfect audio ambiance.

By integrating ChatGPT in VSL creation, you can elevate your storytelling abilities, capture audiences with visually appealing narratives, and drive conversions. Get ready to unleash the full potential of VSLs with the assistance of AI, and watch as your marketing efforts reach new heights.

13

BOOK WRITING

UNLEASHING YOUR CREATIVITY AND AUTHORITY

Books have long been a powerful medium for copywriters to share their expertise, establish authority, and make a lasting impact on readers.

This chapter will consider AI's value throughout the book writing process, from ideation to publication. By utilizing AI tools like ChatGPT, you can unleash your creativity, streamline your writing process, and bring your book to life.

Let's examine the benefits of integrating AI tools throughout the writing process.

Planning and Outlining with AI

Collaborating with ChatGPT, you'll discover how AI can assist in generating book outlines, organizing ideas, and structuring your content effectively. The AI can provide valuable insights, suggest subtopics, and help you refine your book concept, saving you time and enhancing the clarity of your message.

Writing and Editing with AI

ChatGPT can be your virtual writing assistant, generating ideas, improving sentence structure, and enhancing readability. With real-time feedback and suggestions, the AI helps you refine your manuscript and elevate the quality of your writing.

Crafting Compelling Chapters

Delve into the art of crafting engaging chapters that hook readers and keep them captivated. Work with ChatGPT to brainstorm chapter ideas, outline their structure, and infuse them with powerful storytelling techniques that resonate with your target audience.

Designing Book Covers with AI

A visually appealing book cover can attract readers and convey the essence of your content. Learn how to leverage AI tools to design visually appealing book covers that align with your book's theme and grab attention. AI-generated visuals and templates can help you create professional and eye-catching covers without the need for extensive design skills. Here is an example:

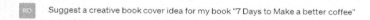 Suggest a creative book cover idea for my book "7 Days to Make a better coffee"

 Book Title: "7 Days to Make a Better Coffee"
Book Cover Idea:
The book cover features a captivating image of a coffee cup on a clean, modern background. The coffee cup is filled with a beautifully layered espresso, showcasing the artistry and craftsmanship behind a perfect cup of coffee. The steam rising from the cup forms the shape of a clock, symbolizing the time-based approach of the 7-day journey. The title "7 Days to Make a Better Coffee" is prominently displayed, with a stylish font that exudes sophistication and expertise. The color palette consists of rich, warm tones, evoking a sense of comfort and indulgence. Overall, the book cover combines visual appeal and a hint of mystery, enticing coffee enthusiasts to embark on a transformative coffee experience.

Publishing and Marketing Strategies

Explore the self-publishing landscape and discover how AI-powered platforms can simplify the process. Learn how to format your book for various digital and print formats with the assistance of AI tools. Additionally, leverage AI-driven marketing strategies, such as keyword research and audience targeting, to maximize your book's visibility and reach the right readers.

Embracing Collaboration

Throughout the book writing journey, it's essential to strike a balance between your creative expertise and AI assistance. AI tools are not here to replace your unique voice but to amplify it, offering fresh perspectives and empowering you to create your best work.

By embracing AI tools like ChatGPT in the book writing process, you can tap into a wellspring of creativity, streamline your workflow, and create a book that resonates with your readers.

Get ready to unleash your creativity and establish yourself as an authoritative voice in your field with the power of AI-assisted book writing.

14

OVERCOMING COMMON AI WRITING CHALLENGES

Artificial intelligence (AI) has undoubtedly revolutionized the field of writing, offering countless benefits and opportunities. However, like any technology, AI writing comes with its own set of challenges.

This chapter will examine common AI writing challenges and strategies for overcoming them. We'll address concerns such as AI bias and inconsistencies, ensuring accuracy and fact-checking, managing tone and voice, and addressing client concerns and expectations.

DEALING WITH AI BIAS AND INCONSISTENCIES

One of the primary challenges with AI writing is the potential for bias and inconsistencies in the generated content. Collaborating with ChatGPT can help you navigate these challenges effectively.

Consider the following strategies.

1. Training Data Diversity: Utilize ChatGPT to ensure that the training data used for the AI model is diverse and representative of various perspectives. By exposing the AI to a wide range of data, you can mitigate bias and improve the generated content's overall quality and fairness.

2. Human Oversight: While AI can assist in generating content, human oversight is essential. Utilize ChatGPT to review and edit the AI-generated content, ensuring it aligns with your values, avoids bias, and meets your specific requirements.

ENSURING ACCURACY AND FACT-CHECKING

Another challenge with AI writing is the need for accuracy and fact-checking. Collaborating with ChatGPT can help you navigate this challenge effectively.

Consider the following strategies.

1. Fact-Checking Resources: Collaborate with ChatGPT to incorporate fact-checking resources into your writing process. The AI can assist in identifying credible sources, verifying information, and suggesting evidence-based content to ensure accuracy.

2. Human Verification: While AI can help generate content, it's vital to have human verification to ensure factual accuracy. Utilize ChatGPT to review and validate the AI-generated content against reliable sources, ensuring that the information presented is correct and up-to-date.

MANAGING TONE AND VOICE

Maintaining a consistent tone and voice is crucial in copywriting. With AI-generated content, it can be challenging to maintain a specific brand voice or writing style. Exploit ChatGPT to address this challenge effectively.

Consider the following strategies.

1. Style Guide: Utilize ChatGPT to create a comprehensive style guide that outlines your brand voice, tone, and writing style. The AI can assist in adhering to these guidelines, providing suggestions and adjustments to ensure consistency across the generated content.

2. Editing and Refinement: Collaborate with ChatGPT to edit and refine the AI-generated content to match your desired tone and voice. The AI can provide alternative wording, phrasing, and suggestions to align the content with your specific style requirements.

ADDRESSING CLIENT CONCERNS AND EXPECTATIONS

You can use ChatGPT to address client concerns and expectations, ensuring client satisfaction.

Consider the following strategies.

1. Transparent Communication: Collaborate with ChatGPT to maintain transparent communication with clients regarding the use of AI in the writing process. Explain the benefits, limitations, and potential challenges of AI-generated content to manage expectations effectively.

2. Sample Reviews: Enlist ChatGPT to provide clients with sample reviews of the AI-generated content. This service allows clients to evaluate the quality and suitability of the content before finalizing the project.

3. Client Feedback Integration: Work with ChatGPT to incorporate client feedback and revisions into the AI-generated content. The AI can assist in incorporating client preferences, making necessary adjustments, and delivering content that aligns with their expectations.

By understanding and addressing common AI writing challenges such as bias and inconsistencies, accuracy and fact-checking, tone and voice management, and client concerns and expectations, you can maximize the benefits of AI writing while ensuring high-quality and tailored content.

15

STAYING AHEAD

CONTINUOUS LEARNING WITH AI TOOLS

In the fast-paced world of copywriting, continuous learning and staying ahead of the curve are essential for success. With the advent of AI tools, copywriters now have powerful resources to enhance their skills and drive better results.

We will now explore the importance of continuous learning with AI tools and how they can help copywriters stay ahead. We'll delve into AI writing tools and resources, harnessing the power of AI in research, using AI for competitive analysis, and keeping up with industry trends.

EXPLORING AI WRITING TOOLS AND RESOURCES

AI writing tools have revolutionized the way copywriters approach their craft. Collaborating with tools like ChatGPT can provide valuable insights, suggestions, and assistance in various aspects of the writing process.

Consider the following ways AI tools can aid in continuous learning.

1. Content Generation: Work with AI writing tools to generate content ideas, outlines, and even full drafts. These tools can help you overcome writer's block, spark creativity, and provide a fresh perspective on your writing.

2. Language Enhancement: AI tools can assist in refining your writing by suggesting alternative word choices, improving sentence structures, and enhancing overall readability. Use AI tools to elevate the quality of your content and expand your linguistic capabilities.

3. Grammar and Style Checks: AI tools can help you identify grammar and style errors in your writing. Use these tools to receive real-time feedback and suggestions for improvement, helping you polish your copy to perfection.

HARNESSING THE POWER OF AI IN RESEARCH

Research is a critical component of copywriting, and AI can be a valuable ally in this process. Collaborating with AI tools for research purposes can provide several benefits, including:

1. Efficient Data Analysis: AI tools can assist in analyzing large volumes of data, extracting relevant insights, and presenting them in a digestible format. With this technology, you can streamline your research process and make data-driven decisions.

2. Topic Exploration: AI tools can help you delve into niche topics by providing comprehensive information, statistics, and expert opinions. Utilize AI tools to expand your knowledge base and gain a deeper understanding of the subjects you write about.

3. Citation and Referencing: AI tools can assist in generating accurate citations and references. Work with these tools to ensure proper attribution and maintain academic integrity in your writing.

USING AI FOR COMPETITIVE ANALYSIS

Understanding your competition is crucial in the copywriting industry. AI tools can provide valuable insights into your competitor's strategies, helping you stay ahead of the game.

Consider the following ways AI can aid in competitive analysis.

1. Social Media Monitoring: AI tools can help you track your competitors' social media activities, engagement metrics, and content performance. Collaborate with AI tools to gain insights into successful strategies, identify trends, and refine your social media presence.

2. Keyword Analysis: AI tools can assist in analyzing your competitors' keyword usage, search rankings, and organic traffic. Utilize AI tools to identify valuable keywords, uncover content gaps, and optimize your copy for improved visibility.

3. Content Analysis: AI tools can help you assess your competitors' content quality, style, and engagement levels. Work with AI tools to gain inspiration, identify areas for improvement, and create content that outshines your competition.

KEEPING UP WITH INDUSTRY TRENDS

The copywriting industry is constantly evolving, so staying informed about the latest trends is essential for success. AI tools can assist in keeping you up to date with industry trends by:

1. Trend Analysis: AI tools can help you identify emerging trends, popular topics, and shifts in consumer behavior. Collaborate with AI tools to understand what resonates with your target audience and adapt your copywriting strategies accordingly.

2. Content Curation: AI tools can assist in curating relevant and trending content from various sources. Make use of AI tools to stay informed about industry news, thought leadership, and best practices, allowing you to provide valuable insights to your audience.

3. Personalized Recommendations: AI tools can provide personalized recommendations based on your preferences and interests. Collaborate with AI tools to receive curated content suggestions tailored to your specific needs, helping you keep your edge in the ever-changing copywriting landscape.

By continuously learning with AI tools, exploring their vast resources, harnessing their power in research and competitive analysis, and keeping up with industry trends, copywriters can position themselves as industry leaders and deliver exceptional results.

16

BUILDING YOUR COPYWRITING BUSINESS WITH CHATGPT

Building a successful copywriting business requires skill, strategy, and leveraging the right tools. With the power of AI, specifically ChatGPT, copywriters can establish a strong brand, price their services effectively, enhance client communication, and scale their business to new heights.

This chapter will explore the steps to building your copywriting business with ChatGPT as your trusted companion.

ESTABLISHING A STRONG COPYWRITING BRAND

A strong brand is essential for standing out in the competitive copywriting industry. Collaborating with

ChatGPT can help you develop and establish a compelling brand identity.

Consider the following strategies.

1. Define Your Unique Value Proposition: Work with ChatGPT to refine and articulate your unique value proposition. The AI can assist in identifying your strengths, differentiating factors, and the specific benefits you bring to clients. This clarity will enable you to position your brand effectively.

2. Craft an Engaging Brand Story: Collaborate with ChatGPT to create an engaging brand story that resonates with your target audience. The AI can help you develop a narrative that showcases your expertise, passion, and the results you've achieved for clients. This story will connect with potential clients on an emotional level.

Craft an Engaging Brand Story of a small Coffee shop run by a retired veteran.

Once upon a time, in a small town, there was a retired veteran named Sam who had a passion for coffee. After serving his country with honor and courage, Sam dreamt of creating a cozy haven where people could gather, connect, and enjoy the perfect cup of joe.

With his retirement savings and a burning desire to pursue his passion, Sam opened a small coffee shop called "Java Junction." The moment customers stepped through the door, they were greeted by the aroma of freshly brewed coffee and a warm smile from Sam.

What made Java Junction unique was not just the high-quality coffee they served, but also the sense of community that permeated every corner of the shop. Sam knew the power of a simple cup of coffee to bring people together, to spark conversations, and to create lifelong friendships.

3. Consistent Branding: Work with ChatGPT to ensure consistent branding across all touchpoints. The AI can assist in creating brand guidelines, including visual elements, tone of voice, and key messaging. Consistent branding establishes trust and reinforces your brand's identity.

PRICING YOUR SERVICES WITH AI ASSISTANCE

Determining the right pricing for your copywriting services is crucial for a profitable business. Collaborating with ChatGPT can assist you in pricing your services effectively.

Consider the following strategies.

1. Competitive Analysis: Work with ChatGPT to analyze industry standards and pricing trends. The AI can help you research what other copywriters are charging for similar services, allowing you to position yourself competitively.

2. Assessing Your Value: Use ChatGPT to evaluate your skills, expertise, and the value you bring to clients. The AI can help you understand the impact of your copy on your clients' business goals. By considering your unique value proposition, you can justify premium pricing.

3. Pricing Structure: Employ ChatGPT to explore different pricing models. The AI can assist in evaluating options, such as hourly rates, project-based pricing, or retainer agreements. Choose a pricing structure that aligns with your business goals and provides flexibility to accommodate various client needs.

RO Make a table of different pricing models for social media copywriting

Certainly! Here's a table outlining different pricing models for social media copywriting:

Pricing Model	Description	Pros	Cons
Hourly Rate	Charging per hour of work	Transparent and flexible	Can be difficult to estimate the total cost for clients
Project-Based	Charging a flat fee for a specific project	Clearly defined scope and cost	May require additional negotiation for scope changes or revisions
Retainer Agreement	Charging a monthly fee for ongoing services	Provides a stable income	Requires a long-term commitment from clients
Performance-Based	Charging based on specific outcomes or results	Aligns with client's goals	Requires clear metrics and tracking system

UTILIZING AI FOR CLIENT COMMUNICATION

Effective client communication is vital for building long-lasting relationships and ensuring client satisfaction. Collaborating with ChatGPT can enhance your client communication processes.

Consider the following strategies.

1. Client Onboarding: Utilize ChatGPT to automate parts of the client onboarding process. The AI can assist in generating welcome emails, questionnaires, and contracts, streamlining administrative tasks, and ensuring a smooth onboarding experience.

2. Customized Proposals: Use ChatGPT to generate customized proposals tailored to each client's specific requirements. The AI can assist in incorporating the client's goals, target audience, and desired outcomes, showcasing your understanding and attention to detail.

3. Real-Time Assistance: Work with ChatGPT to provide real-time assistance during client meetings or calls. The AI can help you generate responses to client queries, provide data-driven insights, and suggest effective solutions to client challenges, enhancing the overall client experience.

SCALING YOUR BUSINESS WITH CHATGPT

Scaling your copywriting business requires efficiency and leveraging the power of AI. Collaborating with ChatGPT can help you scale your business effectively.

Consider the following strategies.

1. Content Repurposing: Collaborate with ChatGPT to repurpose your existing content into different formats, such as blog posts, social media content, or ebooks. The AI can assist in generating new ideas and variations, allowing you to reach a wider audience without investing significant time and effort.

2. Automating Administrative Tasks: Work with ChatGPT to automate repetitive administrative tasks, such as invoicing, contract generation, and project management. The AI can streamline these processes, freeing up time for you to build your business.

3. Outsourcing Support: Use ChatGPT to identify areas where outsourcing can be beneficial. The AI can help you evaluate tasks that can be delegated to virtual assistants or freelancers, allowing you to focus on high-value activities and grow your business strategically.

RO   Write a project briefing for hiring VA for managing social media for a coffee shop.

Project Brief: Hiring a Virtual Assistant for Social Media Management

Project Overview:
We are seeking a skilled and reliable Virtual Assistant (VA) to assist with managing the social media presence of our coffee shop. The VA will play a vital role in enhancing our online presence, engaging with our audience, and driving customer engagement and sales through social media platforms. This project aims to establish a strong social media presence, build brand awareness, and drive traffic to our coffee shop.

Responsibilities:

1. Content Creation: The VA will be responsible for creating engaging and compelling content for our social media platforms, including Facebook, Instagram, and Twitter. This will involve writing captivating captions, designing visually appealing graphics, and scheduling posts for optimal reach and engagement.

By establishing a strong copywriting brand, pricing your services effectively, utilizing AI for client communication, and scaling your business with the assistance of ChatGPT, you can build a thriving and profitable copywriting business.

17

ACQUIRING COPYWRITING CLIENTS

STRATEGIES FOR SUCCESS

I n this chapter, we will explore numerous strategies and techniques to help you attract and acquire copywriting clients.

Whether you're a seasoned professional looking to expand your client base or just starting your journey as a copywriter, these strategies will give you valuable insights and actionable steps to elevate your business.

STRATEGIES TO ATTRACT COPYWRITING CLIENTS

Getting copywriting clients requires a combination of strategic marketing, networking, and showcasing your skills. Here are some effective strategies to attract copywriting clients.

Define Your Target Market

Defining your target market allows you to focus your marketing efforts and tailor your messaging to appeal to specific industries or niches. Research and identify the industries or sectors where your copywriting skills and expertise can make the most impact. By understanding their needs, pain points, and language, you can position yourself as the go-to copywriter in those areas.

Build an Impressive Portfolio

A compelling portfolio is crucial for showcasing your copywriting skills and attracting clients. Select your best work samples that highlight your versatility, creativity, and ability to deliver results. Include a variety of projects across different industries to demonstrate your range. If you're just starting out, consider offering pro bono or discounted services to reputable organizations to build your portfolio.

Optimize Your Online Presence

A professional website or blog allows potential clients to learn more about your services and review your portfolio. Optimize your website for search engines by using relevant keywords, meta tags, and engaging content.

Leverage social media platforms to share your work, engage with your audience, and build a personal brand. Regularly update your online presence to reflect your latest projects and achievements.

Offer Valuable Content

Position yourself as an expert in copywriting by creating and sharing valuable content related to the field. Write blog posts, create videos, or host webinars that provide insights, tips, and strategies to help potential clients with their marketing efforts. Sharing your knowledge demonstrates your expertise, builds trust, and attracts clients who appreciate your value.

Network and Collaborate

Attend industry events, join professional copywriting associations, and participate in online forums or communities. Engage with fellow copywriters, marketers, and potential clients to build relationships, gain referrals, and explore collaboration opportunities. Networking can lead to valuable connections, partnerships, and word-of-mouth recommendations.

Freelancing Platforms

Register on freelancing platforms such as Upwork, Fiverr, or Freelancer to access a wide range of clients actively seeking copywriting services. Create a compelling profile that highlights your skills, experience, and portfolio. Bid on relevant projects that align with your expertise, and deliver high-quality work to build your reputation and attract more clients.

Referrals and Testimonials

Ask satisfied clients for testimonials and referrals. Positive feedback and word-of-mouth recommendations from happy clients can significantly enhance your credibility and attract new clients. Display testimonials prominently on your website and share them on social media to build trust and confidence in your services.

Cold Outreach

Identify potential clients who may benefit from your copywriting services. Research their business and industry to understand their needs and challenges. Craft personalized pitches that address their pain points and highlight the value you can bring to their marketing efforts. Reach out via email, LinkedIn, or other professional networks, demonstrating your expertise and inviting them to explore a collaboration.

Collaborate with Marketing Agencies

Marketing agencies often require copywriting services for their clients. Reach out to agencies that align with your target market or specialize in industries where you excel. Offer to collaborate on projects or be a reliable resource they can outsource to when they need additional copywriting support. Building relationships with agencies can lead to a steady stream of projects and referrals.

Continuous Learning and Improvement

Stay updated on industry trends, best practices, and emerging technologies in copywriting. Attend workshops, take online courses, and invest in your professional development to continuously hone your copywriting skills. Continuous learning allows you to offer the latest strategies and techniques to your clients, positioning yourself as an expert and attracting more high-value clients.

Remember, consistency and perseverance are key when implementing these strategies. Tailor your approach to your target market, communicate your value effectively, and consistently deliver high-quality work. Over time, these efforts will help you attract and retain copywriting clients and build a successful business.

REAL-LIFE STRATEGY: ACQUIRING COPYWRITING CLIENTS FROM LINKEDIN

LinkedIn, the professional networking platform, offers a wealth of opportunities for copywriters to connect with potential clients and showcase their expertise.

By implementing a strategic approach, you can attract copywriting clients on LinkedIn.

Here's a step-by-step strategy, along with a real-life case study.

Step 1: Optimize Your LinkedIn Profile

Make the most of your LinkedIn profile to make a strong impression on potential clients. Use a professional head-shot, craft a compelling headline that highlights your copywriting expertise, and write a concise and engaging summary that showcases your skills, experience, and the value you bring to clients.

Case Study: Sarah, a copywriter specializing in digital marketing, optimized her LinkedIn profile by including relevant keywords in her headline and summary. She highlighted her experience in crafting high-converting copy for various industries and showcased her portfolio through multimedia content.

114 | MARK SILVER

Step 2: Build a Relevant Network

Connect with professionals and businesses in your target market. Search for individuals in marketing, advertising, or related fields who may require copywriting services. Personalize your connection requests to express your interest in their work and how you can add value to their business.

Case Study: John, a copywriter specializing in technology and software, actively sought out connections in the software development industry. He engaged with professionals by commenting on their posts, sharing valuable insights, and offering free resources. This approach helped him build credibility and expand his network.

Step 3: Share Valuable Content

Regularly share valuable content related to copywriting and marketing. Write articles, post informative updates, and share industry news. Provide insights, tips, and strategies that demonstrate your expertise and engage your network. Use relevant hashtags to increase the visibility of your content.

Case Study: Emma, a copywriter specializing in content marketing, shared articles on LinkedIn that offered practical tips for creating engaging content. She used eye-catching headlines and included relevant visuals to make her posts more appealing. This strategy positioned her as an authority in her niche and attracted the attention of potential clients.

Step 4: Engage and Participate

Engage with your network by commenting on their posts, offering thoughtful insights, and initiating conversations. Join relevant LinkedIn groups and actively participate in discussions. By showcasing your knowledge and providing valuable input, you'll establish yourself as a trusted authority in copywriting.

Case Study: Michael, a copywriter specializing in B2B copy, joined LinkedIn groups focused on B2B marketing and sales. He actively participated in discussions, sharing his expertise and providing helpful advice to group members. This engagement allowed him to build relationships and establish credibility with his target audience.

Step 5: Seek and Respond to Opportunities

Keep an eye out for copywriting opportunities posted on LinkedIn. Many businesses and professionals post job openings, freelance projects, or content requests on the platform. Respond promptly and professionally, show-casing your relevant experience and expressing your interest in the opportunity.

Case Study: Lisa, a freelance copywriter, regularly searched for copywriting gigs on LinkedIn. When she came across a post requesting assistance with email marketing copy, she sent a personalized message to the poster, highlighting her experience in email copy-writing and sharing samples of her work. Her timely response and tailored approach helped her secure the project.

By implementing this strategy on LinkedIn, you can attract copywriting clients and expand your professional network. Remember to stay consistent, engage authenti-cally, and provide value to your connections. Each inter-action is an opportunity to showcase your expertise and build relationships that can lead to long-term client part-nerships.

REAL-LIFE STRATEGY: ACQUIRING COPYWRITING CLIENTS THROUGH COLD OUTREACH

Cold outreach, although requiring proactive effort, can be an effective way to acquire copywriting clients. By implementing a well-crafted strategy, you can capture the attention of potential clients and showcase the value you can bring to their businesses.

Here's a step-by-step approach along with a real-life case study.

Step 1: Identify Your Target Audience

Start by identifying your target audience and industries that could benefit from your copywriting services. Research and compile a list of potential clients who align with your niche and need copywriting support.

Case Study: Samantha, a copywriter specializing in digital marketing, identified technology startups as her target audience. She researched and identified companies in the software development industry that could benefit from her expertise in crafting compelling website copy and engaging content.

Step 2: Personalize Your Outreach

Craft personalized and compelling messages for each potential client. Avoid generic templates and demonstrate that you've done your research. Mention specific challenges or opportunities you've identified for their business and how your copywriting skills can help address those.

Case Study: Daniel, a copywriter specializing in the health and wellness industry, personalized his outreach messages by referencing the potential client's recent product launch. He highlighted the importance of persuasive copy in driving customer engagement and offered his expertise in creating captivating marketing content.

Step 3: Choose the Right Channel

Select the most appropriate channel for your outreach, such as email or social media platforms. Tailor your approach based on the preferences of your target audience and the nature of your services. Keep your initial message concise, engaging, and focused on the value you can provide.

Case Study: Emily, a copywriter specializing in e-commerce, chose LinkedIn as her primary outreach channel. She crafted personalized messages to decision-makers in online retail companies, highlighting the impact of compelling product descriptions and engaging website copy on customer conversions.

Step 4: Follow-Up Strategically

Follow up with potential clients after your initial outreach to ensure your message is seen and considered. Craft polite and concise follow-up messages that remind the recipient of your initial contact and reiterate the value you can bring to their business.

Case Study: Benjamin, a freelance copywriter targeting marketing agencies, followed up with potential clients who had expressed interest in his services. He sent personalized follow-up emails, sharing additional success stories and offering to schedule a call to discuss their specific copywriting needs.

Step 5: Showcase Your Expertise

Include samples of your work, case studies, or testimonials in your outreach to demonstrate your expertise and the impact you've made on previous clients. Provide tangible examples of how your copywriting skills have contributed to business growth, increased conversions, or improved customer engagement.

Case Study: Olivia, a copywriter specializing in fashion and lifestyle brands, included links to her portfolio showcasing engaging website copy, captivating product descriptions, and social media campaigns. She also shared testimonials from satisfied clients who had experienced increased sales and brand visibility with her copywriting support.

By implementing a targeted cold outreach strategy, you can acquire copywriting clients and expand your client base. Remember to personalize your messages, demonstrate the value you can bring, and follow up strategically.

Each interaction is an opportunity to build relationships, prove your expertise, and secure long-term partnerships.

SAMPLE 1: COLD OUTREACH EMAIL

Subject: Enhancing Your Brand's Story with Captivating Copywriting

Hello [Client's Name],

I hope this email finds you well. My name is [Your Name], and I am a copywriter specializing in helping brands like yours craft compelling narratives that engage, inspire, and drive results.

I came across [Client's Company] while researching innovative companies in the [Industry/Niche] space, and I was impressed by your commitment to delivering exceptional products/services to your audience. As a copywriter with [X] years of experience, I have worked with various clients in similar industries, helping them create persuasive copy that resonates with their target market.

I would love the opportunity to work with you and assist in elevating your brand's story. Here are a few ways I can help:

1. Website Copy: Engage your visitors from the moment they land on your website with compelling copy that communicates your brand's unique value proposition and converts visitors into loyal customers.

2. SEO-Optimized Content: Enhance your online visibility and attract organic traffic with carefully crafted content optimized for search engines. I can help you create blog posts, articles, and other SEO-friendly content that drives traffic and positions you as an authority in your industry.

3. Social Media Copy: Elevate your social media presence with captivating and shareable content that connects with your audience. I specialize in creating engaging posts that spark conversations, increase brand awareness, and drive user engagement.

I would be happy to discuss your specific copywriting needs and how my expertise can contribute to your brand's success. If you're interested, I would love to set up a call at your convenience to further explore how we can collaborate.

In the meantime, please feel free to visit my portfolio website at [Your Website] to get a glimpse of my previous work and client testimonials. You can also find attached samples of my copywriting for your review.

Thank you for considering my services. I look forward to the possibility of working together and helping you achieve your brand's goals.

Best regards,

[Your Name]

[Your Contact Information]

SAMPLE 2: COLD OUTREACH EMAIL (AIDA MODEL)

Subject: Take Your Brand's Story to New Heights with Compelling Copywriting

Dear [Client's Name],

Are you looking to captivate your audience, drive engagement, and elevate your brand's story? Look no further! I'm thrilled to introduce myself as a copywriter specializing in crafting compelling narratives that leave a lasting impact.

Attention: Grabbing an audience's attention is crucial in today's competitive market. With my expertise in copywriting, I can help you create captivating content that stops readers in their tracks.

Interest: As a copywriter with [X] years of experience, I have worked with numerous clients in [Industry/Niche], delivering exceptional results and driving tangible growth. I came across [Client's Company] and was immediately drawn to your dedication to excellence.

Desire: Imagine having a brand story that resonates with your audience, motivates action, and sets you apart from the competition. With my skills in persuasive copywriting, we can create that desire within your target market and build a strong emotional connection.

Action: Let's take the next step together. I invite you to explore the possibilities of collaborating with me. Whether you need compelling website copy, SEO-optimized content, or engaging social media posts, I have the expertise to help you achieve your goals.

To get a better sense of my writing style and the impact I've made on previous clients, I encourage you to visit my portfolio website at [Your Website]. You'll find samples of my work, along with testimonials from satisfied clients.

I'm eager to discuss your specific copywriting needs and how we can collaborate to enhance your brand's story. Please let me know a convenient time for a call or meeting, and we can dive deeper into your vision and goals.

Don't miss the opportunity to captivate your audience and drive meaningful results with compelling copywriting. I'm here to guide you every step of the way.

Thank you for your time and consideration. I look forward to connecting with you soon.

Best regards,

[Your Name]

[Your Contact Information]

SAMPLE 3: COLD OUTREACH EMAIL (FOLLOW UP)

Subject: Re: Enhancing Your Brand's Story with Captivating Copywriting

Dear [Client's Name],

I hope this email finds you well. I wanted to follow up on my previous message regarding the possibility of collaborating with you to enhance your brand's story through captivating copywriting.

I understand that you are likely busy, and I just wanted to ensure that my previous email didn't get lost in the shuffle. I genuinely believe that my copywriting expertise can make a significant impact on your brand's success.

If you have any questions or require further information, please don't hesitate to reach out. I would be more than happy to discuss your specific copywriting needs and provide additional samples or references if needed.

I truly value the opportunity to work with you and contribute to the growth of your brand. If you are interested in exploring this collaboration further, please let me know, and we can schedule a call or meeting at your convenience.

Thank you for considering my services. I look forward to the possibility of working together and helping you achieve your brand's goals.

Warm regards,

[Your Name]

[Your Contact Information]

SAMPLE 4: LINKEDIN INTRO MESSAGE (CONNECTION REQUEST)

Option: 1

Hi [Connection's Name],

I hope this message finds you well. I couldn't help but notice your impressive work in [industry/field]. As a fellow copywriter, I'm always eager to connect with talented individuals like yourself. It would be great to join forces, share ideas, and support each other in our copywriting endeavors. Let's connect and see what magic we can create together!

Warm regards,

[Your Name]

Option: 2

Hi [Connection's Name],

I am impressed by your work! As a copywriter, I'd love to connect and explore potential collaborations. Let's chat about how we can create compelling content together.

Best,

[Your Name]

SAMPLE 5: LINKEDIN PITCH MESSAGE

Hi [Prospect's Name],

I hope this message finds you well. I noticed that you're in need of high-quality copywriting services, and I wanted to reach out to offer my expertise.

As an experienced copywriter, I specialize in crafting persuasive and engaging content that drives results. Whether you need captivating website copy, compelling blog articles, or attention-grabbing social media posts, I can help your brand stand out and connect with your target audience.

I have a deep understanding of your industry and have successfully worked with clients similar to you. My approach involves thorough research, strategic messaging, and a focus on delivering content that resonates with your audience and achieves your business goals.

I would love the opportunity to discuss your copywriting needs and how I can contribute to your success. If you're interested, I'm available for a quick call or virtual meeting at your convenience.

Looking forward to the possibility of collaborating with you.

Best regards,

[Your Name]

18

STREAMLINING COPYWRITING PROJECTS

MAPPING FOR SPEED AND QUALITY WITH CHATGPT

E fficiency and quality are two key factors that can make or break a copywriting project. In today's fast-paced world, copywriters must deliver exceptional results while meeting tight deadlines.

By leveraging the power of AI, specifically ChatGPT, copywriters can streamline their workflow, enhance creativity, and achieve both speed and quality in their copywriting projects.

Defining Project Goals

Before diving into a copywriting project, it is crucial to clearly define the project goals. This process involves understanding the client's objectives, target audience, and desired outcomes.

By having a clear understanding of what needs to be achieved, copywriters can approach the project with a focused mindset, resulting in more effective copy.

 Client's Brief: Beauty Soap Facebook Ad Copy

Product: Beauty Soap
Target Audience: Women aged 25-45 who prioritize skincare and seek high-quality beauty products.
Goal: Increase brand awareness, drive traffic to the website, and generate product sales.

Gathering Relevant Information

Thorough research is the foundation of compelling copy. Copywriters must gather all the relevant information about the product, service, or topic they are writing about.

This includes understanding the client's brand, target audience demographics, market trends, and any specific guidelines provided. Collaborating with ChatGPT can assist in exploring and organizing the gathered information efficiently.

You can use ChatGPT to gather relevant information based on clients' needs.

Example:

Key Messaging Points:

1. Unique Selling Proposition: Highlight the key features and benefits that differentiate the beauty soap from competitors.
2. Skin Transformation: Emphasize how the beauty soap can improve skin health, clarity, and radiance.
3. Natural Ingredients: Highlight any natural or organic ingredients used in the soap to appeal to conscious consumers.
4. Luxurious Experience: Convey the indulgent and pampering experience of using the beauty soap.
5. Dermatologist Recommended: Mention any endorsements or recommendations from skincare professionals.

Brainstorming Ideas

ChatGPT can be a valuable partner in the brainstorming phase of a copywriting project. By collaborating with AI, copywriters can generate creative ideas, explore different angles, and discover unique selling points.

This collaboration can inspire fresh perspectives and innovative approaches that resonate with the target audience. Use ChatGPT as your brainstorming helper as follows:

1. "Unlock the Secret to Beautiful Skin: Experience the Magic of Our Beauty Soap!"
2. "Indulge Your Skin in Pure Luxury: Discover the Ultimate Beauty Soap Experience!"
3. "Transform Your Skin, Transform Your Confidence: Try Our Beauty Soap Today!"
4. "Experience the Power of Nature: Nourish Your Skin with Our Organic Beauty Soap!"
5. "Elevate Your Skincare Routine: Reveal Radiant Skin with Our Premium Beauty Soap!"
6. "Your Path to Flawless Skin Starts Here: Introducing Our Transformative Beauty Soap!"
7. "Glow from Within: Unleash Your Natural Beauty with Our Skin-Enhancing Beauty Soap!"
8. "Love Your Skin, Love Yourself: Embrace the Beauty of Our Gentle Beauty Soap!"
9. "The Ultimate Skincare Essential: Elevate Your Routine with Our Luxurious Beauty Soap!"
10. "Rejuvenate and Refresh: Unlock Your Skin's Potential with Our Revitalizing Beauty Soap!"

Outlining the Structure

Creating a clear and organized outline is essential for mapping out the copywriting project. By collaborating with ChatGPT, copywriters can structure their copy logically and coherently. The AI can help determine the main sections, key messages, and supporting points, ensuring a well-structured and cohesive copy.

Main Sections:

1. Introduction
2. Key Messages
3. Supporting Points
4. Call-to-Action

Key Messages:

1. Transform Your Skin: Emphasize how the beauty soap can effectively transform the skin's appearance, promoting a healthier, more radiant complexion.
2. Indulge in Luxury: Highlight the luxurious experience of using the beauty soap, evoking a sense of pampering and self-care.
3. Natural Ingredients: Showcase the use of natural and nourishing ingredients in the soap, reassuring customers of its quality and suitability for their skincare needs.

Crafting Compelling Headlines and Hooks

Captivating headlines and hooks are vital for grabbing the reader's attention. ChatGPT can assist in generating attention-grabbing headlines and hooks that resonate with the target audience.

By experimenting with different variations and utilizing AI's suggestions, copywriters can create compelling openings that entice readers to continue engaging with the copy.

Headline 1: "Reveal Your Skin's True Beauty with Our Transformative Beauty Soap!"

Hook: Experience the power of our beauty soap as it nourishes and revitalizes your skin, revealing a radiant and youthful glow that will leave you feeling confident and beautiful.

Headline 2: "Indulge in Pure Luxury: Pamper Your Skin with Our Luxurious Beauty Soap!"

Hook: Treat yourself to a lavish skincare experience with our beauty soap, crafted with the finest natural ingredients to provide a spa-like sensation that leaves your skin soft, supple, and irresistibly touchable.

Developing the Body Copy

The body copy is where the core message is conveyed. Copywriters can work with ChatGPT to develop the body copy, refine the messaging, enhance the flow of ideas, and maintain a consistent tone.

By working together, copywriters and ChatGPT can create persuasive and impactful body copy that resonates with the audience.

Body Copy:
Are you ready to unlock the secret to beautiful, radiant skin? Our transformative beauty soap is here to help you reveal your skin's true beauty. Formulated with the finest natural ingredients and backed by advanced skincare technology, our beauty soap is designed to deliver exceptional results.

Say goodbye to dull, lackluster skin and hello to a complexion that glows from within. Our beauty soap deeply cleanses, removing impurities and excess oil, while brightening and evening out your skin tone. Experience the joy of a refreshed and rejuvenated complexion, as our soap hydrates and moisturizes, leaving your skin feeling soft, supple, and oh-so-smooth.

Editing and Revising

Editing and revising are essential steps in ensuring polished, error-free copy. Copywriters can use ChatGPT to identify grammatical errors, improve sentence structure, and enhance the overall clarity of the copy. The AI's assistance can save substantial time and effort, resulting in a refined and professional final product.

 Proofread following copy:

Body Copy:
Are you ready to unlock the secret to beautiful, radiant skin? Our transformative beauty soap is here to help you reveal your skin's true beauty. Formulated with the finest natural ingredients and backed by advanced skincare technology, our beauty soap is designed to deliver exceptional results.

Say goodbye to dull, lackluster skin and hello to a complexion that glows from within. Our beauty soap deeply cleanses, removing impurities and excess oil, while brightening and evening out your skin tone. Experience the joy of a refreshed and rejuvenated complexion, as our soap hydrates and moisturizes, leaving your skin feeling soft, supple, and oh-so-smooth.

Optimizing for SEO

In today's digital landscape, optimizing copy for search engines is crucial. Copywriters can leverage ChatGPT to identify relevant keywords and incorporate them strategically within the copy. By optimizing for SEO, copywriters can increase the visibility of their copy and drive organic traffic to their client's websites.

 SEO Optimize following text for Keyword: Beauty Soap

Are you ready to unlock the secret to beautiful, radiant skin? Our transformative beauty soap is here to help you reveal your skin's true beauty. Formulated with the finest natural ingredients and backed by advanced skincare technology, our beauty soap is designed to deliver exceptional results.

Say goodbye to dull, lackluster skin and say hello to a complexion that glows from within. Our beauty soap deeply cleanses, removing impurities and excess oil, while brightening and evening out your skin tone. Experience the joy of a refreshed and rejuvenated complexion as our soap hydrates and moisturizes, leaving your skin feeling soft, supple, and oh-so-smooth.

After optimization

 Are you ready to unlock the secret to beautiful, radiant skin with our Beauty Soap? Our transformative beauty soap is specially formulated to help you reveal your skin's true beauty. Made with the finest natural ingredients and backed by advanced skincare technology, our Beauty Soap guarantees exceptional results.

Say goodbye to dull, lackluster skin and say hello to a glowing complexion from within. Our Beauty Soap deeply cleanses, eliminating impurities and excess oil, while also brightening and evening out your skin tone. Experience the sheer delight of a refreshed and revitalized complexion as our soap deeply hydrates and moisturizes, leaving your skin irresistibly soft, supple, and incredibly smooth.

Testing and Iterating

Collecting feedback and testing the effectiveness of the copy is integral to the copywriting process. By collaborating with ChatGPT, copywriters can gather insights and iterate on their copy based on feedback received. This iterative approach allows for continuous improvement and ensures the copy meets and exceeds client expectations.

Finalizing and Delivering

Once the copy has been refined and meets all the project goals, it is time to finalize and deliver the completed copy to the client. Collaborating with ChatGPT for final proofreading can catch any last-minute errors or inconsistencies, ensuring a flawless and professional end product. With their copy finalized and delivered, copywriters can celebrate a job well done.

Mapping out copywriting projects with the assistance of ChatGPT can significantly improve efficiency and enhance the quality of the final copy. By following these steps, copywriters can streamline their workflow, generate creative ideas, and approach their projects with a clear roadmap for success.

The combination of human creativity and AI-powered assistance empowers copywriters to deliver exceptional results that captivate audiences and drive desired outcomes.

19

SUCCESS STORY

VERBALVANTAGE COPYWRITERS

John, the founder of VerbalVantage Copywriters, leveraged the power of ChatGPT to transform his copywriting business into a thriving enterprise that generates a six-figure income per month.

By specializing in social media copywriting and utilizing the capabilities of ChatGPT, John was able to achieve remarkable success.

Here are the key factors that contributed to his achievement.

Establishing VerbalVantage Copywriters

- **Identified a Niche:** John recognized the growing demand for social media copywriting and positioned VerbalVantage as a specialist in this field.
- **Defined Brand Values:** By collaborating with ChatGPT, John crafted a compelling brand story that conveyed VerbalVantage's expertise, commitment to quality, and ability to deliver results.
- **Consistent Branding:** With the AI's assistance, John ensured that VerbalVantage's branding was consistent across all channels, reinforcing its identity and building trust with clients.

Pricing Strategies and Client Acquisition

- **Competitive Pricing:** Collaborating with ChatGPT, John conducted thorough market research to determine competitive pricing that aligned with VerbalVantage's value proposition.
- **Value-Based Pricing:** Leveraging the AI's insights, John highlighted the unique value his

team offered, allowing VerbalVantage to charge premium rates based on the quality and impact of their social media copy.

- **Targeted Marketing:** With ChatGPT's assistance, John optimized VerbalVantage's marketing efforts by identifying and targeting ideal clients through data-driven strategies, increasing their acquisition rate.

AI-Assisted Client Communication

- **Efficient Onboarding:** ChatGPT helped John streamline client onboarding by automating the generation of welcome emails, questionnaires, and contracts, ensuring a seamless experience for clients.
- **Real-Time Assistance**: During client interactions, John relied on ChatGPT for real-time assistance, providing prompt and accurate responses to queries. By doing so, he demonstrated VerbalVantage's professionalism and commitment to client satisfaction.
- **Personalized Approach**: The AI's insights enabled John to tailor VerbalVantage's communication to each client's specific needs and goals, fostering strong client relationships and repeat business.

Scaling Operations with ChatGPT

- **Content Repurposing:** Collaborating with ChatGPT, John repurposed existing social media copy into various formats, optimizing their efficiency and reaching a broader audience without compromising quality.
- **Automating Administrative Tasks:** The AI assisted John in automating repetitive administrative tasks such as scheduling, invoicing, and project management, allowing VerbalVantage to handle more projects with increased efficiency.
- **Strategic Outsourcing:** ChatGPT helped John identify areas where outsourcing certain tasks, such as graphic design or content distribution, could accelerate VerbalVantage's growth, freeing up his time for higher-value activities.

By harnessing the power of ChatGPT and focusing on social media copywriting, John transformed VerbalVantage Copywriters into a lucrative business, generating a substantial six-figure monthly income.

His success story highlights the immense potential of AI in the copywriting industry, offering aspiring entrepreneurs like John the opportunity to achieve remarkable financial prosperity while delivering exceptional value to clients.

EMMA'S STORY

Emma, a struggling freelance copywriter, experienced a remarkable turnaround in her financial situation by leveraging her expertise in writing video sales letters on platforms like Upwork and Fiverr.

Starting from a position of financial struggle, Emma honed her skills and utilized the power of persuasive storytelling to generate a substantial income. Last month, she earned an impressive $4,763 solely through her video sales letter writing services.

Here's how Emma achieved this transformation.

Refining Her Craft

- **Commitment to Skill Development:** Emma dedicated herself to mastering the art of writing persuasive and engaging video sales letters. She invested time and effort in studying successful VSLs, learning from industry experts, and continually improving her copywriting techniques.

- **Collaboration with ChatGPT:** Emma partnered with ChatGPT to refine her writing skills further. The AI provided valuable insights, offered suggestions for effective storytelling and pacing, and assisted in generating compelling hooks and calls to action for her video sales letters.

Building an Online Presence

- **Creating a Professional Profile:** Emma established a robust online presence on platforms like Upwork and Fiverr, showcasing her expertise in video sales letter writing. She crafted a professional profile that highlighted her experience, skills, and successful track record, instilling confidence in potential clients.
- **Showcasing a Portfolio:** Emma worked with ChatGPT to create an impressive portfolio of her past work. The AI helped her compile engaging snippets and key highlights from her video sales letters, demonstrating her ability to capture attention and drive conversions.

Effective Client Communication

- **Compelling Proposals:** Emma utilized ChatGPT to generate customized proposals tailored to each client's needs. The AI provided her with insights into the client's target audience, goals, and desired outcomes, allowing her to create persuasive and relevant proposals.
- **Timely and Professional Communication:** Emma understood the importance of prompt and professional client communication. She responded to inquiries quickly, provided clear and concise information, and collaborated with ChatGPT to ensure her responses were well-crafted and aligned with the client's expectations.

Delivering Exceptional Results

- **Crafting Engaging Video Scripts:** Emma's expertise in storytelling and persuasive copywriting allowed her to create video scripts that drew viewers and compelled them to take action. She worked with ChatGPT to fine-tune her scripts, ensuring they were emotionally resonant, concise, and tailored to the client's product or service.

- **High Conversion Rates:** Emma's video sales letters consistently delivered impressive results for her clients. The persuasive copy she crafted, coupled with compelling visuals, drove higher conversion rates and increased sales for their businesses.

Emma's story is a testament to the transformative power of leveraging one's skills, embracing AI collaboration, and utilizing online platforms to generate a substantial income.

By focusing on video sales letter writing, honing her craft, and leveraging the capabilities of ChatGPT, Emma turned her financial situation around and achieved remarkable success.

Her dedication, talent, and strategic approach enabled her to earn $4,763 last month, cementing her position as a sought-after expert in video sales letter copywriting.

FUTURE OF COPYWRITING

AI AND BEYOND

The future of copywriting is intricately intertwined with the rapid advancements in artificial intelligence (AI). As AI continues to evolve, it brings exciting opportunities and challenges for the copywriting industry.

In this chapter, we'll explore the evolving trends in AI copywriting, discuss the importance of ethics and responsibility in AI usage, provide insights on preparing for the future of AI copywriting, and emphasize the significance of embracing AI as a valuable copywriting tool.

Evolving Trends in AI Copywriting

AI copywriting has come a long way, and its potential for growth and innovation is vast. As we look to the future, several key trends are shaping the landscape of AI copywriting.

1. **Natural Language Generation (NLG):** NLG technology allows AI models to generate human-like text with remarkable fluency. This trend opens doors for more sophisticated AI-generated copy that closely resembles human-written content.

2. **Hyper-Personalization:** AI-powered algorithms and data analysis enable copywriters to create hyper-personalized content tailored to individual users. By leveraging AI tools, copywriters can deliver customized messaging that resonates deeply with their target audience.

3. **Multilingual Capabilities:** AI is continuously improving its ability to understand and generate content in multiple languages. Copywriters can leverage AI-powered translation and localization tools to create content that seamlessly caters to global audiences.

4. **Content Optimization:** AI tools can analyze vast amounts of data and provide insights into content performance, user engagement, and conversion rates. Copywriters can leverage these insights to optimize their

copy, enhance audience targeting, and improve overall effectiveness.

Ethics and Responsibility in AI Usage

As AI becomes more prevalent in the copywriting industry, it's essential to uphold ethical and responsible practices.

Consider the following factors to ensure ethical AI usage.

1. Bias Mitigation: AI models can inadvertently perpetuate biases present in the data they are trained on. Copywriters should use AI tools like ChatGPT to actively mitigate biases and ensure fair, inclusive content generation.

2. Transparency and Disclosure: It's crucial to be transparent with audiences when AI is involved in content creation. Clearly disclosing your use of AI-generated content builds trust and fosters open communication with your audience.

3. Data Privacy and Security: Copywriters must prioritize data privacy and security when utilizing AI tools. Collaborate with trusted AI platforms that prioritize privacy measures and adhere to data protection regulations.

Preparing for the Future of AI Copywriting

To prepare for the future of AI copywriting, consider the following strategies:

1. Continuous Learning: Embrace a growth mindset and commit to continuous learning. Stay updated with the latest AI advancements, industry trends, and best practices through professional development, courses, and networking with other copywriters.

2. Adapting to Change: Be open to change and embrace new technologies as they emerge. Copywriters who adapt quickly to evolving AI tools and techniques will have a competitive advantage in the industry.

3. Collaboration with AI: Foster a collaborative relationship with AI tools like ChatGPT. Understand their capabilities, leverage their strengths, and use them as valuable resources to enhance your copywriting skills and deliver exceptional results.

Embracing AI as a Valuable Copywriting Tool

Rather than viewing AI as a threat, copywriters should embrace it as a valuable tool in their arsenal. AI can augment and amplify their creative capabilities, improve efficiency, and deliver high-quality content.

Embracing AI can lead to the following benefits.

1. Increased Productivity: AI tools can automate repetitive tasks, allowing copywriters to focus on high-value activities. Delegating minutiae to AI boosts productivity and enables copywriters to deliver more impactful copy in less time.

2. Enhanced Creativity: AI-generated suggestions and insights can spark new ideas and inspire copywriters to think outside the box. Collaborating with AI tools like ChatGPT can foster a symbiotic relationship between human creativity and AI-generated assistance.

3. Improved Accuracy and Consistency: AI tools can help maintain consistency in brand voice, tone, and style across various content pieces. They can also assist in identifying grammatical errors, ensuring high-quality and error-free copy.

As we look to the future, the symbiotic relationship between copywriters and AI tools will continue to shape the copywriting industry. By understanding and embracing the evolving trends, upholding ethics and responsibility, preparing for the future, and harnessing the power of AI as a valuable tool, copywriters can thrive in the dynamic and exciting world of AI-powered copywriting.

AI is not a replacement for copywriters but a powerful ally that can enhance their skills, streamline their processes, and unlock new possibilities.

By embracing AI and its capabilities, copywriters can elevate their craft, deliver exceptional content, and stay at the forefront of the copywriting industry.

SPREAD THE WORD!

With AI at its disposal, copywriting has an exciting future ahead – and this is your chance to spread the word.

Simply by sharing your honest opinion of this book and a little about your own experience with AI, you'll show new readers where they can find everything they need to know to harness its power.

Thank you for your support, and the best of luck in your copywriting career.

CONCLUSION

In this comprehensive guide, we have explored the power of AI in copywriting and how it can revolutionize the way we create content. We started by understanding the rise of AI in copywriting and the advantages it brings to the table. Overcoming the fear of automation is a vital step, as AI is meant to assist and enhance our abilities rather than replace us.

Mastering the basics of copywriting is also essential before diving into the world of AI-assisted writing. We delved into the fundamentals of copywriting, emphasizing the power of persuasion and crafting compelling headlines and hooks.

Understanding our audience is another crucial factor in creating effective copy.

We then introduced ChatGPT, your AI writing partner, and discussed its benefits for copywriting. ChatGPT becomes a valuable tool as we explore strategies for effective AI-assisted writing. Collaborating with ChatGPT speeds up the writing process and generates ideas and outlines. It streamlines content creation and editing, allowing for a more efficient workflow.

Perfecting our craft with ChatGPT involves leveraging the AI's capabilities for grammar and style, improving clarity and readability, incorporating emotional appeal, and enhancing creativity. We explored writing advertisements, creating persuasive sales pages, and optimizing ad performance, highlighting the power of AI in the realm of marketing.

Moving forward, we explored the use of ChatGPT for content marketing, email marketing, SEO copywriting, social media copywriting, video sales letters, book writing, and overcoming common AI writing challenges. We provided insights and strategies for each area, empowering copywriters to excel with AI assistance.

Continuous learning with AI tools becomes a focal point in staying ahead. Harnessing AI for research, competitive analysis, and keeping up with industry trends helps copywriters remain at the forefront of their field.

Building a copywriting business with ChatGPT involves establishing a strong brand, pricing services with AI assistance, utilizing AI for client communication, and scaling the business effectively.

We then delved into strategies for acquiring copywriting clients, sharing real-life examples and samples for cold outreach and LinkedIn communication. These strategies equip copywriters with the tools they need to expand their client base.

To illustrate the potential of AI in copywriting, we shared the success story of VerbalVantage Copywriters, focusing on Emma's journey to demonstrate the transformative power of AI.

Finally, we explored the future of copywriting, acknowledging that AI is just the beginning. As technology advances, the possibilities for copywriters will continue to expand.

With this comprehensive guide, copywriters can embrace AI as a powerful tool to enhance their skills, streamline their processes, and create outstanding content. By understanding the power of AI in copywriting and harnessing its capabilities, the future of copywriting is limitless.

ABOUT MARK SILVER

Mark Silver (aka *The AI Entrepreneur*) is a serial entrepreneur, investor, and innovator. His mission is to make people wealthy by sharing knowledge, information and investment opportunities, and new ways to make money online with one million people.

By changing their lives, he can impact billions of people. An obstacle for many people is money. He plans to remove that burden with his books, courses, and programs so more people can focus on their true purpose and passions.

ALSO BY MARK SILVER

The AI Entrepreneur Series

CHATGPT PROMPTS

SEO Copywriting:

1. "Write an SEO-friendly meta description for a blog post about [specific technique]."
2. "Craft a compelling title tag for a webpage targeting [long-tail keyword]."
3. "Develop an introduction paragraph optimized for [target keyword] in an industry-related article."
4. "Create keyword-rich alt text for images on a website dedicated to [your subject]."
5. "Write a persuasive call-to-action (CTA) at the end of a landing page focused on [target keyword]."
6. "Craft a headline for a product category page that entices users and includes relevant keywords."
7. "Develop SEO-focused bullet points for a product description of [specific item]."
8. "Write a captivating meta title for a local business page targeting [location] customers."
9. "Create engaging subheadings for an in-depth SEO guide on [specific technique or strategy]."
10. "Craft keyword-rich anchor text for internal links on a webpage related to [your industry]."
11. "Write an attention-grabbing H1 tag for a webpage discussing [important topic in your niche]."
12. "Develop an SEO-friendly URL structure for a blog post about [specific subject]."
13. "Create optimized image file names for visuals on a website focusing on [your industry]."
14. "Craft a compelling meta description for a service page targeting [specific audience]."

15. "Write a keyword-rich header tag (H2 or H3) for an article on [relevant topic]."

16. "Develop a concise and informative meta description for a product page featuring [specific item]."

17. "Craft SEO-friendly anchor text for external links in a resource list on [your subject]."

18. "Write an enticing title tag for a landing page promoting a free [resource or tool]."

19. "Create keyword-rich alt text for infographics on a website specializing in [your industry]."

20. "Develop a meta title for a blog post about the future of [your industry/niche]."

21. "Craft a compelling meta description for a landing page promoting [specific product/service]."

22. "Write an attention-grabbing H1 tag for a comprehensive guide on [industry-related topic]."

23. "Develop SEO-focused bullet points for a product comparison page highlighting [specific features]."

24. "Create keyword-rich anchor text for backlinks in an industry resource roundup article."

25. "Craft a persuasive meta title for a case study showcasing the success of [client/company]."

26. "Write an informative introduction paragraph for a whitepaper discussing [emerging trend]."

27. "Develop SEO-friendly subheadings for a long-form blog post on [specific subject]."

28. "Create engaging meta descriptions for a series of blog posts on [industry-related topic]."

29. "Craft a keyword-rich H2 tag for a webpage addressing frequently asked questions about [your product/service]."

30. "Write a compelling title tag for a landing page promoting a free webinar on [relevant topic]."

Book Writing:

1. "Craft an intriguing book title that captures the essence of your story or subject matter."
2. "Develop an engaging book cover blurb that entices readers to dive into your book."
3. "Write an attention-grabbing opening chapter that hooks readers from the very first page."
4. "Create relatable and memorable characters that readers will connect with throughout your book."
5. "Craft compelling dialogue that brings your characters to life and drives the narrative forward."
6. "Develop vivid descriptions of settings and environments that transport readers into your book's world."
7. "Write a captivating climax that leaves readers on the edge of their seats, eager to know what happens next."
8. "Create an emotionally resonant ending that satisfies readers and leaves a lasting impression."
9. "Craft engaging chapter titles that pique readers' curiosity and foreshadow what's to come."
10. "Write a thought-provoking prologue or introduction that sets the tone for your book."
11. "Develop a compelling back cover synopsis that summarizes your book's main conflict and stakes."
12. "Create compelling subplots that add depth and complexity to your book's narrative."
13. "Craft realistic and multi-dimensional villains or antagonists that challenge your protagonist."
14. "Write impactful and memorable quotes or passages that resonate with readers long after they've finished your book."
15. "Develop an immersive and well-researched historical or fantasy world for your book's setting."
16. "Create unexpected plot twists and turns that keep readers guessing and engaged."

17. "Craft a compelling character arc that shows growth and transformation throughout your book."
18. "Write authentic and relatable dialogue that reflects the unique voices of your characters."
19. "Develop a captivating middle section that maintains momentum and builds towards the climax."
20. "Create a satisfying resolution that ties up loose ends and leaves readers with a sense of closure."

Social Media Copywriting:

1. "Write a captivating Facebook post introducing a new product or service offering."
2. "Craft a tweet highlighting a customer testimonial or success story about your brand."
3. "Develop an engaging Instagram caption for a visually striking photo showcasing your product."
4. "Create a LinkedIn post discussing the latest industry trends and offering valuable insights."
5. "Write a persuasive caption for a Pinterest pin promoting a collection of your products."
6. "Craft a Facebook ad copy targeting a specific audience segment for your product or service."
7. "Develop an attention-grabbing headline for a YouTube video demonstrating your product in action."
8. "Create an Instagram story inviting followers to ask questions about your industry or expertise."
9. "Write a tweet introducing a blog post that offers valuable tips or advice on a relevant topic."
10. "Craft a LinkedIn headline highlighting the unique benefits of your product or service for professionals."
11. "Develop an engaging caption for an Instagram carousel post showcasing different uses of your product."

12. "Create a Facebook post announcing a partnership or collaboration with another brand or influencer."
13. "Write a persuasive caption for an Instagram post inviting followers to join a webinar or live event."
14. "Craft a tweet promoting a limited-time offer or discount on a specific product or service."
15. "Develop a LinkedIn post discussing the impact of recent industry news or updates on businesses."
16. "Create an attention-grabbing headline for a Facebook Live session addressing common challenges in your industry."
17. "Write an engaging caption for an Instagram post featuring a customer review or testimonial about your product."
18. "Craft a tweet introducing a new feature or enhancement to your product or service."
19. "Develop a LinkedIn post showcasing a valuable resource or whitepaper related to your industry."
20. "Write an Instagram caption inviting followers to participate in a giveaway or contest."

Email Marketing Copywriting:

1. "Craft an attention-grabbing subject line for a welcome email series for new subscribers."
2. "Write a persuasive opening paragraph for an email newsletter introducing a limited-time offer or promotion."
3. "Develop a personalized email copy for a special birthday discount or gift for loyal customers."
4. "Create a follow-up email subject line for an abandoned cart reminder campaign to encourage conversions."
5. "Write an informative email introducing a new feature or upgrade to your product or service."
6. "Craft a compelling CTA for an email encouraging users to register for an upcoming webinar or event."

7. "Develop an email copy for a product launch announcement targeting existing customers."

8. "Create an enticing subject line for an exclusive discount or early access offer for your subscribers."

9. "Write a persuasive testimonial request email to gather feedback and reviews from satisfied customers."

10. "Craft an engaging email subject line for a newsletter featuring industry insights, tips, and trends."

11. "Develop an email copy for a customer re-engagement campaign offering a special incentive or discount."

12. "Write a personalized email introducing a new loyalty program and its benefits to customers."

13. "Craft an attention-grabbing subject line for an email showcasing customer success stories and case studies."

14. "Create an email copy promoting a limited-time bundle or package deal on your products or services."

15. "Write a persuasive opening paragraph for an email campaign introducing a new blog post or resource."

16. "Develop an email copy for a referral program, encouraging customers to refer friends and earn rewards."

17. "Craft an enticing subject line for a flash sale or clearance event in your online store."

18. "Write an informative email introducing a new educational guide, e-book, or course on a relevant topic."

19. "Create a persuasive CTA for an email campaign inviting subscribers to participate in a survey or poll."

20. "Develop an email copy for a post-purchase follow-up campaign, asking for product reviews and offering related recommendations."

Landing Page Copywriting:

1. "Write a compelling headline that grabs the reader's attention and communicates your unique value proposition."
2. "Craft an introductory paragraph that clearly outlines the benefits and advantages of your product or service."
3. "Develop a persuasive subheading that highlights a key feature or solves a specific problem for your audience."
4. "Create a compelling call-to-action (CTA) that prompts visitors to take the desired action on your landing page."
5. "Write customer testimonials or success stories that provide social proof and build trust with your audience."
6. "Craft a bulleted list of key benefits and features that clearly communicate the value of your offering."
7. "Develop a visually appealing infographic or graphic element that visually represents your offering or data."
8. "Create a comparison table that highlights how your product or service outperforms the competition."
9. "Write a persuasive closing paragraph that reinforces the urgency or scarcity of your offer."
10. "Craft a testimonial or review widget that dynamically displays positive feedback from satisfied customers."
11. "Develop a FAQ section that addresses common questions or concerns your audience may have."
12. "Create a compelling headline and description for a lead magnet or free resource to incentivize sign-ups."
13. "Write a persuasive guarantee or refund policy that eliminates risk and builds trust with potential customers."
14. "Craft a visually appealing video or animated element that engages and educates visitors about your offering."
15. "Develop a visually appealing pricing table that showcases different package options and their features."
16. "Create a compelling exit-intent pop-up that offers a special discount or bonus to encourage conversions."

17. "Write a persuasive headline and subheading combination that addresses a pain point and offers a solution."
18. "Craft a visually striking testimonial carousel that rotates through positive customer feedback and reviews."
19. "Develop a countdown timer or urgency indicator that creates a sense of scarcity and encourages immediate action."
20. "Create a visually appealing progress bar that showcases the steps or stages of your offering or onboarding process."

Ad Copywriting:

1. "Write a captivating headline for a Facebook ad promoting your product or service."
2. "Craft a compelling opening sentence that hooks viewers' attention in a YouTube pre-roll ad."
3. "Develop an attention-grabbing visual or image for an Instagram ad showcasing your offering."
4. "Create a persuasive call-to-action (CTA) that drives users to click on your Google Ads search ad."
5. "Write a punchy tagline for a banner ad that encapsulates the essence of your brand or offering."
6. "Craft a headline and description combination for a LinkedIn ad targeting professionals in your industry."
7. "Develop an engaging opening scene or scenario for a video ad introducing your product or service."
8. "Create a visually appealing carousel ad for Facebook or Instagram showcasing different product variations."
9. "Write a persuasive value proposition statement for a display ad on a relevant industry website."
10. "Craft a headline and subheading combination for a native ad that seamlessly blends with the editorial content."
11. "Develop an attention-grabbing opening line for a Twitter ad promoting your latest blog post or resource."

12. "Create a visually striking GIF or animation for a display ad that captures users' attention."

13. "Write a persuasive description for a Google Ads remarketing ad targeting users who visited your website."

14. "Craft a headline and subheading combination for a retargeting ad that addresses users' pain points."

15. "Develop an engaging testimonial or review ad featuring a customer's positive feedback and results."

16. "Create a visually appealing product-focused ad showcasing the unique features and benefits."

17. "Write a compelling call-to-action (CTA) for a YouTube video ad that drives users to subscribe or visit your website."

18. "Craft a headline and description combination for a Facebook carousel ad highlighting different customer success stories."

19. "Develop an attention-grabbing opening scene or visual for a video ad promoting a limited-time offer or sale."

20. "Create a persuasive headline and description for a Pinterest ad showcasing your product or service in an inspirational context."

Video Sales Letter Copywriting:

1. "Write a compelling opening statement that captures viewers' attention and introduces your product or service."

2. "Craft an engaging story or narrative that resonates with viewers and showcases the problem your offering solves."

3. "Develop a powerful value proposition that clearly communicates the unique benefits and advantages of your offering."

4. "Create visually appealing visuals or animations that support your message and enhance the viewer's understanding."

5. "Write a persuasive call-to-action (CTA) that encourages viewers to take the next step in the sales process."

6. "Craft customer testimonials or case studies that provide social proof and build trust with viewers."

172 | CHATGPT PROMPTS

7. "Develop a visually appealing product demonstration that showcases the features and functionality of your offering."
8. "Create a compelling offer or bonus that adds value and creates a sense of urgency for viewers."
9. "Write a persuasive closing statement that summarizes the key benefits and reinforces the value of your offering."
10. "Craft an attention-grabbing headline and subheading combination that highlights the main problem and solution."
11. "Develop an engaging visual or graphic element that visually represents the transformation your offering provides."
12. "Create an emotionally impactful soundtrack or background music that enhances the overall tone and mood of your video."
13. "Write a powerful testimonial or success story from a satisfied customer that showcases the results they achieved."
14. "Craft an engaging script that follows a logical flow and addresses common objections or concerns viewers may have."
15. "Develop visually appealing text overlays or captions that highlight key points and reinforce your message."
16. "Create a visually striking before-and-after comparison that illustrates the positive impact of your offering."
17. "Write a persuasive value stack or breakdown that showcases the value and savings viewers can expect."
18. "Craft an attention-grabbing opening hook or question that piques viewers' curiosity and keeps them engaged."
19. "Develop a visually appealing transition or animation between different sections or key points in your video."
20. "Create a compelling visual or graphic that represents your money-back guarantee or risk-free trial offer."

E-commerce Copywriting:

1. "Write a persuasive product description that highlights the features and benefits of [specific product]."
2. "Craft an attention-grabbing headline for a homepage banner promoting a limited-time sale or discount."
3. "Develop compelling bullet points for a product listing that emphasize key selling points."
4. "Create an engaging email subject line for an abandoned cart recovery campaign to encourage conversions."
5. "Write a persuasive call-to-action (CTA) for a product page that prompts visitors to make a purchase."
6. "Craft a captivating product title and description for a new arrival in your online store."
7. "Develop a visually appealing infographic showcasing the uses and benefits of your product."
8. "Create a compelling banner ad copy for a retargeting campaign targeting users who viewed your product."
9. "Write an attention-grabbing headline for a product category page that sparks curiosity."
10. "Craft a persuasive product comparison guide that helps customers make an informed buying decision."
11. "Develop an email copy for a product launch announcement, highlighting its unique features and benefits."
12. "Create a visually appealing video script for a product demo that showcases its functionality."
13. "Write a compelling headline and subheading combination for a product testimonial or customer review."
14. "Craft a persuasive CTA for a checkout page that encourages upselling or cross-selling."
15. "Develop engaging blog post titles for content that educates and informs customers about your products."
16. "Create a visually appealing packaging copy that reflects your brand's values and appeals to customers."

17. "Write an enticing social media post promoting a flash sale or exclusive discount for your products."
18. "Craft an attention-grabbing headline for a pop-up offer inviting visitors to sign up for your newsletter."
19. "Develop an engaging FAQ section that addresses common customer queries about your products."
20. "Create a persuasive landing page copy that highlights the unique selling points of your products."

Public Relations Copywriting:

1. "Write a captivating press release headline for a new product or service launch."
2. "Craft an attention-grabbing opening paragraph that introduces the key news or announcement."
3. "Develop a compelling media pitch that highlights the newsworthy aspects of your company or brand."
4. "Create an engaging company boilerplate that summarizes your brand's mission and achievements."
5. "Write a persuasive executive bio for a key spokesperson or company leader."
6. "Craft a captivating quote from a company representative that adds credibility and impact to a press release."
7. "Develop a crisis communication statement that addresses and manages a potential PR issue or incident."
8. "Create an informative fact sheet that provides key details about your company, product, or event."
9. "Write a compelling media advisory or invitation for an upcoming press conference or event."
10. "Craft a persuasive blog post that positions your company as a thought leader in your industry."
11. "Develop an engaging email pitch to journalists or influencers, showcasing the value of your story."

12. "Create a visually appealing media kit that includes high-resolution images, company background, and press releases."
13. "Write a compelling company announcement for a significant milestone or achievement."
14. "Craft a persuasive social media post promoting a recent press coverage or feature."
15. "Develop an impactful brand story that connects with your target audience and resonates with the media."
16. "Create a captivating case study highlighting the success and impact of your product or service."
17. "Write a persuasive sponsorship proposal that outlines the benefits and opportunities for potential sponsors."
18. "Craft a compelling award nomination submission that showcases your company's accomplishments and contributions."
19. "Develop an engaging newsletter highlighting recent media mentions and news updates."
20. "Create a visually appealing infographic showcasing key statistics or industry insights related to your brand."

B2B Copywriting:

1. "Write a persuasive headline for a B2B landing page that captures the attention of your target audience."
2. "Craft a compelling opening paragraph that highlights the pain points and challenges faced by B2B professionals."
3. "Develop an informative whitepaper title that addresses a relevant industry topic or trend."
4. "Create an engaging email subject line for a B2B lead generation campaign targeting decision-makers."
5. "Write a persuasive call-to-action (CTA) for a B2B product or service page that encourages inquiries or requests for a demo."
6. "Craft a captivating case study headline that showcases the success and results achieved for a B2B client."

7. "Develop a visually appealing infographic highlighting key industry statistics or research findings."

8. "Create a compelling testimonial from a satisfied B2B client that highlights the impact of your product or service."

9. "Write a persuasive proposal introduction that clearly articulates the value and benefits of your offering."

10. "Craft an attention-grabbing headline and subheading combination for a B2B blog post or thought leadership article."

11. "Develop an informative FAQ section that addresses common questions and concerns raised by B2B prospects."

12. "Create a visually appealing presentation deck for a B2B sales pitch or webinar."

13. "Write a persuasive social media post promoting a B2B webinar, workshop, or industry event."

14. "Craft a captivating headline for a B2B newsletter that highlights industry insights and updates."

15. "Develop an engaging email series for B2B lead nurturing, educating prospects about your offering."

16. "Create a visually appealing infographic showcasing the benefits and features of your B2B solution."

17. "Write a compelling headline and description for a B2B e-book or industry guide."

18. "Craft a persuasive CTA for a B2B landing page that encourages visitors to download a resource or schedule a call."

19. "Develop an informative FAQ section that addresses common questions and objections raised by B2B prospects."

20. "Create a visually appealing testimonial video featuring a B2B client discussing the positive impact of your solution."

Brand Copywriting:

1. "Write a captivating brand tagline that encapsulates the essence and values of your company."
2. "Craft an attention-grabbing brand mission statement that communicates your purpose and goals."
3. "Develop a compelling About Us page copy that tells the story of your brand and engages your audience."
4. "Create an engaging brand manifesto that defines your brand's philosophy and resonates with your target audience."
5. "Write a persuasive brand story that connects with customers on an emotional level and builds brand loyalty."
6. "Craft a captivating brand voice guide that outlines the tone, language, and personality of your brand."
7. "Develop an impactful brand positioning statement that differentiates your brand from competitors."
8. "Create a visually appealing brand style guide that includes logo usage, color palette, and typography guidelines."
9. "Write a compelling brand value proposition that highlights the unique benefits and advantages of your products or services."
10. "Craft an attention-grabbing headline for a brand-focused blog post or content piece."
11. "Develop a persuasive brand ambassador program description that invites influencers to represent your brand."
12. "Create a visually appealing brand mood board that captures the aesthetic and visual identity of your brand."
13. "Write a compelling brand partnership proposal that outlines the mutual benefits and opportunities for collaboration."
14. "Craft an engaging brand manifesto video that showcases your brand's vision and impact."
15. "Develop an informative brand presentation that communicates your brand story and positioning to internal stakeholders."
16. "Create a persuasive brand sponsorship deck that highlights the alignment between your brand and potential sponsors."

17. "Write a captivating brand manifesto letter that introduces your brand to customers and invites them to join your journey."
18. "Craft a compelling headline and description for a brand-focused social media post or campaign."
19. "Develop an impactful brand activation idea that creates a memorable and immersive brand experience for your audience."
20. "Create a visually appealing brand brochure or booklet that show-cases your brand's offerings, history, and values."

Technical Copywriting:

1. "Write a clear and concise user manual or guide for a technical product or software."
2. "Craft an attention-grabbing headline for a technical blog post or article addressing a specific problem or solution."
3. "Develop an informative FAQ section that addresses common technical questions and troubleshooting tips."
4. "Create a persuasive product description for a technical gadget or tool that highlights its features and functionality."
5. "Write a compelling case study showcasing the successful implementation of a technical solution for a client."
6. "Craft an engaging technical whitepaper title that explores an emerging trend or innovation in your industry."
7. "Develop an informative glossary of technical terms and acronyms for your website or resource hub."
8. "Create a visually appealing infographic that simplifies complex technical concepts or processes."
9. "Write a persuasive call-to-action (CTA) for a technical landing page that encourages downloads or sign-ups."
10. "Craft an attention-grabbing headline and subheading combination for a technical webinar or online training session."
11. "Develop an informative data sheet or specification document that outlines the technical specifications of your product or service."

12. "Create a visually appealing technical diagram or flowchart that illustrates a complex process or system."
13. "Write a persuasive email campaign promoting a technical webinar, demo, or industry event."
14. "Craft a captivating headline and description for a technical podcast episode or video tutorial."
15. "Develop an engaging script for a technical explainer video that simplifies a complex concept or process."
16. "Create an informative comparison chart that highlights the features and benefits of different technical solutions."
17. "Write a compelling headline and description for a technical e-book or industry report."
18. "Craft a persuasive CTA for a technical support page that guides users to seek assistance or submit a ticket."
19. "Develop an engaging email series for onboarding new users and guiding them through your technical product or platform."
20. "Create a visually appealing troubleshooting guide or knowledge base article that helps users resolve common technical issues."

Please note that these prompts are meant to provide inspiration and guidance for copywriting in each category. Feel free to modify or adapt them to suit your specific needs and objectives.

REFERENCES

Anand, S. (2022, July 5). 40 best artificial intelligence quotes Blogs &
   Updates on Data Science, Business Analytics, AI Machine Learning.
   https://www.analytixlabs.co.in/blog/40-best-artificial-intelligence-
   quotes/

Made in the USA
Coppell, TX
24 February 2024

29375682R00105